WILD ABOUT
Richmond
& KEW

THE THAMES, THE PARK, THE GARDENS

By Andrew Wilson
& Caroline MacMillan

Sponsored by

CHESTERTONS

I would like to dedicate my latest book to my historian, Caroline, and her husband Colin. We met by pure chance four years ago and this is our fifth book together and we already have plans for a sixth – thanks Caroline.

St Helena Terrace, Friar's Lane and Riverside

FOREWORD BY BAMBER GASCOIGNE

One of the great merits of Richmond is that it has made almost no concessions to the car – compare the travesties of Croydon or Kingston. The only exception is the A316, slicing through the Old Deer Park in the 1930s and separating Richmond from Kew. Apart from that, the centre of the town still has the informal layout seen in John Rocque's map of London in 1746, a pattern of lanes and narrow roads with no straight lines. It is a perfect small town to walk in. After 50 years I still haven't been able to work out the shortest route between places I often visit.

Those 50 years have seen a massive change in the condition of the town rather than in its geography. The buildings between the bridge and Water Lane were then mostly derelict and several of them empty. There was a glorious moment in 1975 when Erin Pizzey, famous at the time for her work with battered wives, arrived in the night with a group of distressed women and children to take over one of the buildings as a squat. Word whizzed round and Richmond rose to the occasion; large amounts of furniture, bedding and food turned up on the following day.

And there has been a very great change in the nature of the town. There were few visitors then, even to the riverside which in Edwardian times was a thriving scene with scores of people in small rowing boats on a day out from London (beautiful large hats on the ladies). Now it has a life and bustle of its own again, partly because of the return of boatbuilding with the arrival of Mark Edwards (designer and builder of Gloriana) in the 1990s – but also as a result of the beautiful green sloping lawns near the bridge in place of the previous dereliction. Richmond is once again the most popular place for an outing on a warm summer's evening, with the riverside and local pubs teeming with visitors having a good time, most of them young.

The most regretful change, true of so many places, is in the nature of the shops. George Street is now full of major retail stores. Fifty years ago the very short King Street, leading off the Green, had two rival butchers and a privately owned cookery shop (the desk on which the till sat had stationed beneath it the manager's pet parrot, which could be heard gnawing away at the wood until a new desk was required). Now the only surviving traditional shop in the street is the brilliant Open Book, owned by Helena Caletta whose faithful following enables her to survive within fifty yards of a big Waterstone's.

Richmond's greatest glories, the Park, the Hill, Petersham Meadows, the Terrace Gardens, the River, the historic Green with its superb 18th-century houses, and Kew Gardens survive just as they always have and are beautifully brought to life in Wild about Richmond. Time to visit Helena.

Since we first published our book, Bamber Gascoigne
has sadly passed away (February 2022).

3

Clockwise from top left: Richmond Bridge, Richmond Park, Richmond Green and St Anne's, Kew Green.

Contents

Welcome to Wild About Richmond & Kew

Welcome to the second edition of my 14th book in my ever-expanding series of books on the villages and towns of south and west London. There hasn't been time to update the content, so some of the shops have sadly gone but most of the rest is very much as it was. However, it is sad to note that Bamber Gascoigne, who kindly supplied such a colourful foreword to the book, passed away in February 2022. A lovely man and it was only recently that I discovered that back in the 80's he published something very similar to this and it was a shame I never got to discuss this with him.

I live relatively close to Richmond and it was only a matter of time before I covered this glorious part of our wonderful city. I thought I knew the area quite well, but I was still surprised by many new things, so the wonderful autumn colour on The Green, to discovering places I didn't even know existed, the allotments down Old Palace Lane for instance.

My books take well over a year to produce and with all my books, there are many people along the way who have helped me and none more so than my historian, Caroline MacMillan. This is our fifth book together and her energy is quite infectious and I look forward to our next 'campaign'. Besides being a historian, Caroline is also a local guide and as with our previous projects together, we have included within the book three walks, which is our way of transporting you out of the book and into the very streets so that you could find out for yourself what a wonderful place this is. Then there are my sponsors, Chestertons. I was introduced to Xavier, from their Richmond office, by the manager in Barnes who I know well and I was so pleased when he immediately took to the idea of supporting a project of this size and complexity. To help spread the load, he kindly talked Daniel from their Kew office into helping us. Since the first edition, we have continued to work together, and I produce a calendar for them each year. I would like to thank Angela Ivey, from Visit Richmond, who

I have known for some years; wherever I went there she was, promoting the delights of the borough. By coincidence, one of my friends, Julia Stead, happens to be one of the organisers for Richmond Hill Open Gardens and I am grateful to her and her colleagues for allowing me to feature some of their private gardens within the book. Thankfully, we were blessed with a beautiful day back in May 2017. As well as the gardens, there are many other places featured in the book and wherever possible I have tried to thank as many of the people I have met along the way as possible within the text. Finally, I would like to thank my designer, Kieran Metcalfe, who has kindly helped me with this second edition. I love photography and I pinch myself every warm and sunny day that I am out and about with my camera that this is my work. Many people say to me that the sun is always shining in my books and I hope my book brings a little light into your world.

Andrew Wilson
2022

Josie – on the left Richmond Hill and right, Richmond Park at sunset

Richmond & Kew

A SHORT HISTORY OF RICHMOND
by Caroline MacMillan

Glide gently, thus forever glide,
O Thames! that other bards may see,
As lovely visions by thy side
As now, fair river! come to me.

Lines Written near Richmond, Upon the Thames

Below: The royal barge, *Gloriana*, which was built locally and headed the 1000-strong flotilla for the Queen's Diamond Jubilee in 2012.

So wrote William Wordsworth in 1790. Like many poets and artists, he was captivated by the beauty of the Thames as it flowed endlessly passed the river banks of Richmond and Petersham's meadows. The same river would have been familiar to Anglo-Saxon fishermen living in huts by the water's edge and after 1066, to the Norman family of Belet who built a substantial manor house overlooking the Thames. In those days the hamlet was known as Syenes, the origin of which probably lay in the Anglo-Saxon word sceo meaning 'shelter' and this in turn evolved into Shene. In the fourteenth century the manor reverted to royal hands and Edward III built himself a palace, The Palace of Shene, where his grandson, Richard II, later brought his young bride. It soon became their favourite residence but he was so distraught when she died there of the plague, that he ordered its demolition. Henry V and his successor Henry VI between them built a new and larger palace but following a disastrous fire in 1497 it was left to Henry VII to rebuild it in even grander style. He decreed it should be known as the Palace of Richmond, named after his favourite earldom in Yorkshire. The riverside palace continued to be favoured by royalty: Elizabeth I died there in 1603 and Charles I often hunted deer in the Great Park, the present Richmond Park, which he enclosed with a high brick wall. However, after his execution, Parliament sold the palace and most of the buildings were demolished.

Due to the presence of the court, the village of Richmond was a prosperous one. The palace always had need of additional staff such as embroiderers and seamstresses, cooks and bakers, whilst taverns sprang up to provide meals and overnight accommodation for visitors. From the end of the 17th century rich merchants were attracted by its proximity to the capital and invested in land where they built summer houses – Clarence House in the Vineyard and The Rosary and The Hollies in nearby Ormond Road date from this period.

The East View of King Henry VII Palace, on Richmond Green.

The next hundred years saw more grand villas and mansions built along the river and on the slopes of the hill. A former Lord Mayor of London, Sir Charles Asgill, commissioned the elegant house with its prime river frontage which still carries his name, whilst Sir Joshua Reynolds built Wick House at the top of the hill from where he painted the view, this being his only major landscape painting.

Over the centuries the rich were generous in looking after the less fortunate. The oldest charity is the Church Estate whose almshouses overlook Sheen Road. Queen Elizabeth's Almshouses were founded in 1600, whilst those of Bishop Duppa who was tutor to the Prince of Wales, later Charles II, were built as a thanksgiving when his former pupil was restored to the throne. William Hickey's charity provided homes and pensions of £4 per annum for six poor men and ten poor women and sisters Rebecca and Susanna Houblon were the benefactors of the almshouses which stand on Worple Way. The parish too addressed the problem and the first workhouse was set up in 1729, being replaced by a larger one on Grove Road some fifty years later.

The first house of religion was the Shene Charterhouse founded by Henry V in 1414. It was the largest and richest of pre-Reformation Carthusian houses in the country and flourished until the dissolution of the monasteries by Henry VIII. Tucked away behind two busy roads the parish church of St. Mary Magdalene stands in an oasis of calm. James Thomson who wrote the lyrics of "Rule, Britannia" is buried near the front, whilst the landmark spire of Sir George Gilbert Scott's Gothic style church dedicated to St. Mathias, can be seen from miles around from its position on Richmond Hill. The Roman Catholic church of St. Elizabeth in the Vineyard was built and paid for by Miss Elizabeth Doughty who lived nearby on The Terrace. The Wesleyans established their theological college on Richmond Hill in 1843, followers have attended services at the Ebenezer Strict Baptist church in Jocelyn Road since 1897. The Bethlehem Chapel, tucked away in Church Terrace, was built a century earlier and is believed to be the oldest Independent Free Church in west London still being used as a place of worship.

The earliest mention of a school at Richmond can be found in a document dated

VIEW FROM RICHMOND BRIDGE.

Now and then: View downstream from Richmond Bridge today and from early last century. Thanks to all the staff from the Local Studies department within the local library for helping me source the old pictures featured here and within the book.

1581 which mentions one for the choristers of the Chapel Royal. A charity school was set up in 1713 attached to the church of St. Mary Magdalene and informally called the Bluecoat school. This tradition continues today with the blue blazors worn by pupils of Christ's School, as it is now known. Since 1867 when it was founded in the road of that name, Vineyard School continued to expand and in the 1970s

moved to new premises on Richmond Hill. During the 18th and 19th centuries numerous private schools were established in the town, one being the Richmond Academy which opened in a mansion overlooking Little Green in 1764, its most famous pupil being explorer and writer, Sir Richard Burton. A century later it was a Cavalry College but following a fire the house was rebuilt, renamed Onslow Hall

and is now occupied by Barclays Bank. The gothic style castellated exterior of Ellerker College on Richmond Hill was founded by Mrs. Yarrow in 1889 and is home to The Old Vicarage School.

With the discovery of a mineral spring on the hillside in the 1670s the well-to-do travelled from London, by river or horse and carriage, to 'take the waters' and enjoy the pleasure garden, pump room, assembly and gaming rooms which developed around it. There had been no theatrical performances at Richmond since Queen Elizabeth's time but the New Theatre opened on Richmond Green in 1765 with the comic opera "Love in a Village" and the renowned actor Edmund Kean was theatre manager for the last two years of his life. This Georgian theatre was demolished in 1884 and Frank Matcham, the leading theatre architect of the day, was commissioned to design a new one overlooking Little Green which opened on the 18th September 1899 with a performance of Shakespeare's "As you Like it". Soon talking pictures were capturing the public's gaze and Richmond's first cinema arrived in 1910 when the former Castle Assembly Rooms were converted to accommodate the Castle Electric Theatre. The now listed Odeon on Hill Street opened in 1930 with an auditorium designed to evoke a Spanish nobleman's 17th century house and courtyard.

Over the centuries the beauteous delights of Richmond have attracted many from the world of the arts. Geoffrey Chaucer was familiar with Shene Palace having been appointed Yeoman of the King's Chamber in 1368, and the playwright and poet Richard Brinsley Sheridan lived at Downe House on Richmond Hill more than 400 years later. Charles Dickens often spent summer months at Petersham and marked the publication of David Copperfield with a dinner at the Star and Garter Hotel which was attended by William Thackeray and Alfred, Lord Tennyson. Virginia Woolf and her husband Leonard were residents for nine years from 1914 and established The Hogarth Press in their house in Paradise Road. As well as Reynolds, Thomas Rowlandson was entranced by this idyllic stretch of the Thames and produced some charming vignettes including one of Asgill House with the beau monde promenading before it. In later years Spencer Gore lived in Cambrian Road and painted many landscapes in Richmond Park. Musicians too found their way to Richmond; Johann Christian Bach, known as the 'London Bach', had a house in Richmond in the 1770s, Gustav Holst once lived in Grena Road and in more recent times members of the Rolling Stones and The Who have made their home here.

Top: Roebuck Pub on Richmond Hill

Now and then: Richmond Bridge from Cambridge Gardens, from 1895 and today.

Now and then: Bridge Street today and from around 1910.

Since the first palace was built, Richmond's major industry has been catering for its visitors. The many ale houses and taverns of Elizabethan times have long gone including the charmingly named Lily Pot on the corner of Brewers Lane, but eighteenth century drinkers would have known The Roebuck which was an alehouse in 1717 and also The Cricketers where beer has been served since 1741. One of the most famous hostelries was the Star and Garter at the top of Richmond Hill. It started life in 1738 as a modest tavern and flourished to reach its peak of fame as a hotel in Victorian times but the final building designed in French chateau style closed in 1907 and the Star and Garter Home for Disabled Sailors, Soldiers and

Airmen was built on the site. In 2014 the Grade II listed building with its iconic view of the Thames valley was sold and has now been turned into luxury apartments.

Richmond has never been a market town due to a charter granting Kingston a monopoly within a seven mile radius. In Tudor times the first shops clustered around the Green, over the years spreading up King Street and along the west side of what is now George Street. This is where Gosling's drapery opened in 1795 and remained until 1968 when the site was redeveloped by Dickens and Jones, now the House of Fraser. By 1851 Charles Mayne had a thriving green grocery business employing 60 men and women, Martha Bull could be relied upon for tripe and Frederick Newby was a hawker of eggs and butter. From 1880 Messrs. Hornby and Clarke's herd of cows grazing on nearby Petersham meadows supplied their outlets in south west London with dairy products. A magnificent example of one of their shops still exists on Richmond Hill, though no longer as a dairy. The well established City firm of wine and spirit merchants, Ellis & Co., relocated to Hill Street in 1920 and planted a vine outside their premises which produced grapes for many years. The most famous of Richmond shops is surely number 3 Hill Street where, early in the eighteenth century, the famous Maids of Honour tartlets were first made to a recipe which remains secret to this day.

Despite protestations from watermen concerned at loss of income, the ferry between Richmond and the Twickenham meadows was replaced by an elegant stone bridge in 1777, the eighth Thames bridge across the river in London. From the eighteenth century this stretch of the river hosted magnificent Royal Regattas with brass bands entertaining spectators and the day ending with bursts of fireworks. Although many of the boat houses have now found other uses, wooden craft continue to be made here; master craftsman Mark Edwards led the team who built the magnificent rowing barge *Gloriana*, which was at the head of the flotilla of a thousand boats sailing down the Thames for the Diamond Jubilee of Queen Elizabeth II. Cholmondeley Walk is a favourite place to stroll and watch swans and boats on the river, a scene as familiar to the Victorians as it is to visitors today. One of the most recent additions to Richmond's river's vista is the Quinlan Terry riverside development where listed buildings have been preserved and combined with new ones, in a variety of Georgian and classical styles, to form a daisy-chain of picturesque and impressive architecture.

The age of steam arrived at Richmond by river in 1816 when a daily steamer service operated between London Bridge and Richmond. For visitors to the town twelve years later a single fare was 1s 3d (one shilling and three pence), approximately £5.00 in today's money and whilst passengers enjoyed pleasant views on their journey, it

had drawbacks if the wind was in the wrong direction and they were engulfed by black smoke. The first train reached the town in 1846 at a station located between Kew Road and Parkshot but as the network expanded a new station was required and the familiar Art Deco one we see today opened in 1937.

Richmond continued to be favoured by royalty and after William III enlarged the hunting lodge in the Old Park, Richmond Lodge became a much enjoyed country retreat for subsequent monarchs. Richmond attracted nobility too, the Duke of Ancaster's mansion stood outside Richmond Park's walls across the road from the Star and Garter tavern, whilst the gardens of the Duke of Buccleuch's riverside house on the Petersham boundary were the

scene of a spectacular fete when Queen Victoria visited in 1842. But the arrival of the railway was also the beginning of a new era for the town. The early Victorian rows of workmen cottages were now joined by medium sized villas for middle class Londoners who commuted to London by train, estates sprang up and the new road names – Ellerker, Mount Ararat and Hermitage – reflected those of the grand houses on whose grounds they now stood.

As the twentieth century dawned, Edwardian Richmond continued to prosper as fashionable Londoners enjoyed a day by or on the river, but change was on the horizon. The First World War saw houses on the Green converted for military hospital use and early planes including Sopwith 'Pups' built by the Whitehead Aircraft

Company at their Townshend Terrace works. During the next World War air-raid shelters were constructed on the Green which was a wise precaution as the town endured some substantial bombing, with the Town Hall being badly damaged during one raid. Modern times have seen more housing developments, new shops opening along the already busy shopping streets and office blocks to which workers now commute to Richmond.

Richmond has grown beyond all recognition since fishermen built their huts here but what has remained constant is the Thames as it timelessly weaves its way past the town's banks. Alaric Watts in his 'Lyrics from the Heart' captures this magic.

Caroline MacMillan, 2017

Let poets rave of Arno's stream,
And painters of the winding Rhine,
I will not ask a lovelier dream,
A sweeter scene, fair Thames, than thine;
As, in a summer's eve decline,
Thou "glidest at thine own sweet will",
Reflecting from thy face divine
The flower-wreathed brow of Richmond Hill!

Alaric Watts 'Lyrics from the Heart'

Card kindly provided by The Francis Frith Collection

Left: Postcard from 1955

Richmond & Kew

A SHORT HISTORY OF KEW
by Caroline MacMillan

Nestling in a sweeping bend of the River Thames, Kew has grown from a small hamlet, where early inhabitants earned their living from fishing the waters and farming the land, to a substantial London suburb now famed for two of the country's most important institutions, the Royal Botanic Gardens and the National Archives. In 54 BC Julius Caesar wrote a detailed account of his second raid on Britain and records there was only one place some seventy miles inland where the river was fordable, and whilst historians continue to debate the exact location, the short crossing between Kew and Brentford is regarded as being the most likely place. Kew's name derives from Saxon times when it was known as Cayho meaning a quay (Cay) on a spur of land (ho) and in the 1314 Survey of the Manor of Shene, there is mention of 'Gilbert of Cyho' holding 18 acres of farmland and two acres of meadow there.

After Edward III built his palace at Shene and then Henry VII his even larger one which he duly named Richmond, the ford at Kew was replaced by a ferry and business was good for local boatmen and trade in general. During the Tudor period courtiers wishing to be close to the Richmond royal court found Kew a convenient place to live. The rival dukes of the king-making families of Somerset and Northumberland plotted at their Kew homes, whilst it is said that Queen Elizabeth I visited her favourite, Robert Dudley, Earl of Leicester at his property there. Kew became home to royalty itself when Frederick, Prince of Wales, acquired Kew Park, already known for its exotic garden. William Kent was appointed to enlarge and improve the house, which was named the White House so as to distinguish it from the red brick Dutch House facing it across the Green. The Prince was a passionate gardener

Above: The Barn Church, Atwood Avenue

and continued to develop the existing gardens but it was his son, George III, who in 1759 recruited William Aiton from the Chelsea Physic Garden to take charge. Together with Joseph Banks, they fulfilled the Prince's dreams.

By 1759 the ferry had given way to a wooden bridge and this in turn was replaced by a stone one some twenty years later. The river continued to aid Kew's prosperity and especially that of the boatmen, whilst farmers found it more profitable to grow fruit and vegetables on the fertile meadows where an acre of asparagus would reap ten times that for a similar amount of wheat. When the railway arrived in 1869 the number of visitors to the botanical gardens increased dramatically and restaurants and tea shops, some offering overnight accommodation, opened in the elegant Georgian houses around the Green. Flourishing until the 1940s, today only the Newens' Maids of Honour shop in nearby Kew Road remains and continues selling their famous tartlets made to a secret recipe.

Until 1714 the village was without a church but after a group of local dignitaries pledged financial contributions and Queen Anne donated the land, a simple chapel of ease was built which was tactfully dedicated to the saint bearing her name. Some 60 years later the chapel became a church when George III paid Joshua Kirby to expand the building and seating arrangement in order to accommodate the increase in both the local population and his own family. Tucked away in Atwood Avenue is the church of St. Philip and All Saints, the first church in England to be built from a barn. The beams of a 17th century barn in Surrey, which were possibly timber from ships of Armada times, were carefully dismantled and numbered and brought here in 1929 and then reassembled. It is still possible to see the numbers painted on the wood.

Times were changing in Kew. The railway had opened the way for many more visitors and in 1904 its close link with royalty came to an end when the Duke of Cambridge died and his house on the Green was given to the Gardens. By the end of the 1920s the fertile market garden land belonging to the Selwyn, Taylor and Leyborne Popham estates had been sold and homes for commuters to London now lined the streets, some of which were named after former landowners. The market gardeners went too but other businesses took their place and in 1892, Viscose, an artificial silk later called rayon, was discovered by two chemists in a little cul-de-sac off Sandycombe Road. Visitors to the Gardens continued to increase, offering more employment opportunities to Kewites and when in 1977 the National Archives moved their records dating back more than a thousand years to

their new home by the river, so even more visitors flocked to this former village on the bend of the river.

But some things have remained constant, such as the tranquility of Kew's riverside as the Thames slips quietly by and the beauty of the Green, particularly on a sunny Sunday afternoon, with the sound of leather on willow and applause from spectators enjoying a game of cricket, as so many have done since Frederick, Prince of Wales attended "a great cricket match" on 27th July 1732.

Now and then: South Circular Road as it passes through Kew Green.

The River

Linking the City of London with Windsor and Hampton Court, lying to the west of Richmond, the river has provided a living to watermen and boat builders for centuries. The river has attracted day visitors for many a year, such as in 1772 when the Master, Wardens and Assistants of the Worshipful Company of Stationers and their ladies traveled by barge to Richmond, and were duly entertained at the Star and Garter before returning to the City. The annual Richmond Regatta attracts thousands of spectators as does the September Great River Race, held on a 21-mile course from Greenwich to Ham and regarded as London's river marathon. More than three hundred crews participate ranging from serious racers to an assortment of vessels including longboats, dragon boats and novelty crafts and although it is exhausting for the rowers, it is a spectacular sight for those watching from the river's banks.

Having founded Chelsea Football Club with his brother Gus, Joseph Mears acquired the Thames Electric & Motor Launch Company on Eel Pie Island in 1907 and went on to become one of the main operators of passenger launches on the river. Basing his headquarters in Richmond, he also had a fleet of motorised coaches, built several cinemas in the Richmond area and became Mayor of the town in 1931.

The Kingwood was built for him in 1915 and is one of the Little Ships of Dunkirk, having taken part in Operation Dynamo and the rescue of more than 338,000 British and French soldiers trapped on that French beach in 1940. To this day, she continues to carry passengers enjoying a day out on the Thames at Richmond. Whilst watermen rowed boats which carried passengers, lightermen rowed 'lighters' which were flat bottomed barges used for moving goods. In 1835 the St. Helena boathouses were let to the three major Richmond lightermen families of Downs, Jackson and Wheeler who used them for storage of freight and coal.

Richmond is twinned with three cities from around the world, Richmond Virginia in the US, Konstanz in Germany and Fontainebleau in France. As well as the many cultural links that have taken place over the years, no doubt helped by the 'champion' we have within the council, we all share another major and more natural phenomenon, we are all close to or on rivers.

Above: The Great River Race each year attracts over 300 boats and in 2010 even included a Viking ship.

Richmond Bridge

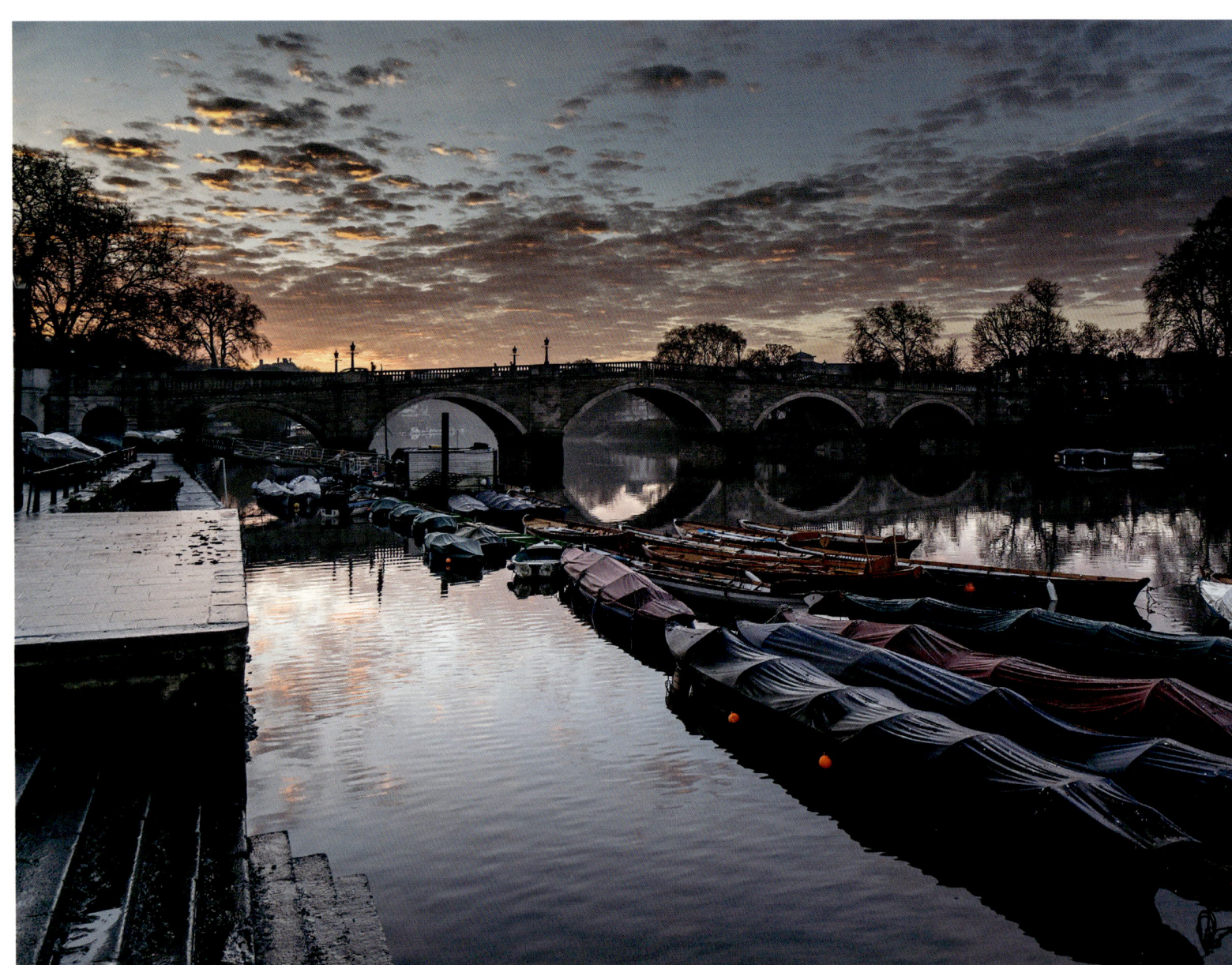

The first stone for Richmond Bridge was laid by Henry Hobart in 1774. There was no formal opening ceremony when the first pedestrians walked across in September 1776, with vehicles using it from the following January. Construction was financed by the issue of tontine shares, a system whereby the interest from toll charges was divided amongst the surviving holders of non-transferable shares. The last subscriber died in March 1859 and two weeks later the bridge became toll free, the toll houses were demolished and the alcoves where they once stood became seating areas. The bridge is the only remaining Georgian one spanning the Thames in London.

Bottom right: The river and Richmond Bridge, 1900

Opposite: The Bridge in the snow of 2012. It hasn't snowed that much in recent years.

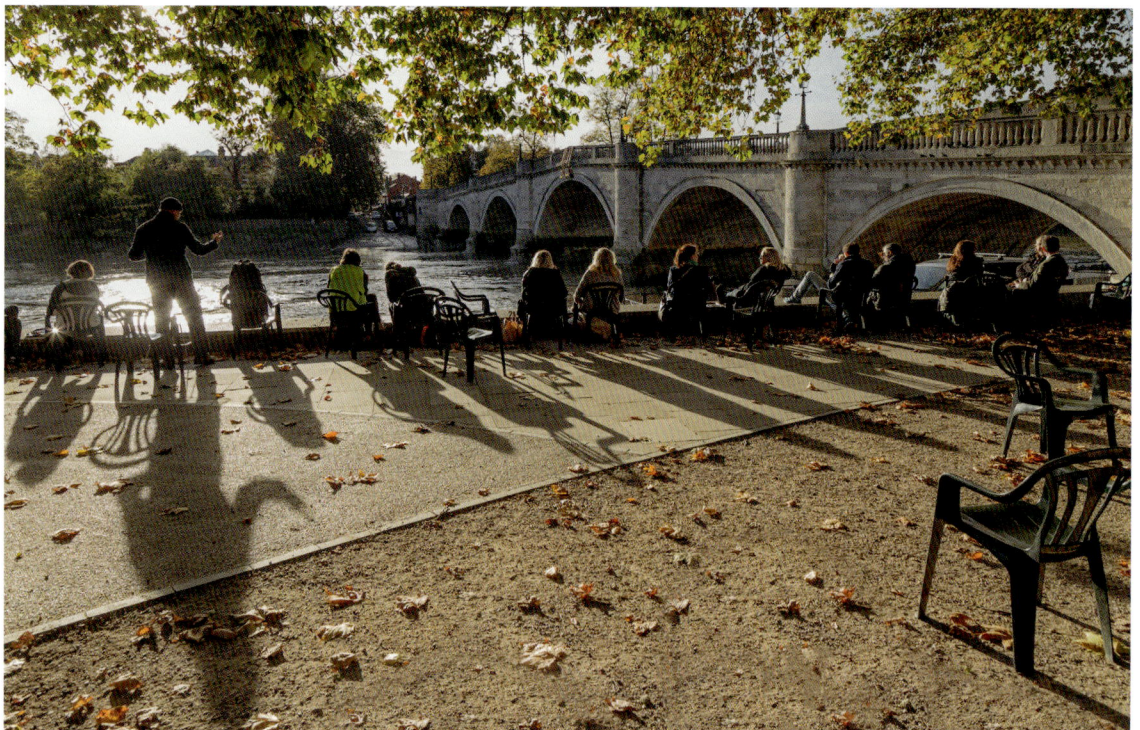

Bottom left: The Tide Tables Café. Literally found under the arches of the bridge, the café is a popular haunt for both locals and tourists, especially as its on the Thames Path, which makes it a wonderful stopping off point for the many walkers who stroll by. It has a sister establishment, The Hollyhock Café, in nearby Terrace Gardens.

Opposite: Richmond Bridge is not the only bridge spanning this part of the river. Standing on Twickenham Bridge (this page, bottom right) you can view The Railway Bridge (bottom left) and The Footbridge by the lock and weir (top left).

The railway bridge we see today was completed in 1908 but incorporated much of the fabric of the original one of 1848, which had been one of the earliest rail bridges constructed across the Thames. The bridge together with the handsome brick viaduct extending into Old Deer Park were declared a Grade II listed structure in 2008.

Twickenham Bridge: The construction of the so-called 'Great Chertsey Road' through Richmond in the 1930s (though the road never got as far as Chertsey) required the demolition of many old houses and cottages along the Lower Mortlake Road, whilst the southern tip of Old Deer Park lost ground in order to accommodate the new Twickenham Bridge. The proposed design for this bridge included four 70 foot towers on the riverbanks, with retaining walls some 20 feet above road level, and it was therefore widely opposed for being inappropriate for the setting in Richmond. The final design of three reinforced concrete arches supported on concrete piers with art deco decoration also incorporates three permanent hinges which enable the structure to adjust to changes in temperature. It is the first reinforced concrete bridge in the UK to use this innovation. It was opened by the Prince of Wales in 1933 after which the much-needed widening of Richmond Bridge was put in hand.

The Riverfront

Top right: Statue to General Bernardo O'Higgins found just off the approach to the bridge. Born in Chile, Bernardo was the illegitimate son of Ambrosio O'Higgins, a Spanish officer born in County Sligo, Ireland who later became Viceroy of Peru. At the age of seventeen he was sent to England to complete his studies and lived at Clarence House, which at that time was a Catholic school. Returning to Chile he was instrumental in freeing the country from Spanish rule and is considered one of Chile's founding fathers.

There are more than a dozen London plane trees, or *Platanus x Hispanica* as they are known to aborists, growing along Richmond's river embankment but one of them at more than 50 metres (164 feet) has a plaque declaring it is the tallest of its kind in the capital and a Great Tree of London. Although, there are some who say that one of the two planes at the bottom of Old Palace Lane is taller but I'm not sure how one might check.

This Page: Italianate style Tower House was built by Henry Laxton in 1856 and remained a private residence until the 20th century. By 1930 it was Nuthall's Restaurant with the owner living in a flat in the upper floors of the tower.

Opposite: The Christmas Market – having an outdoor market in late November can be a precarious thing, however in 2016 it was a lovely day. I like my art, especially photography of course, but it was pleasure to meet the guys from The Jolly Creative Workshop (bottom right), who create wonderful original pieces using old printing methods.

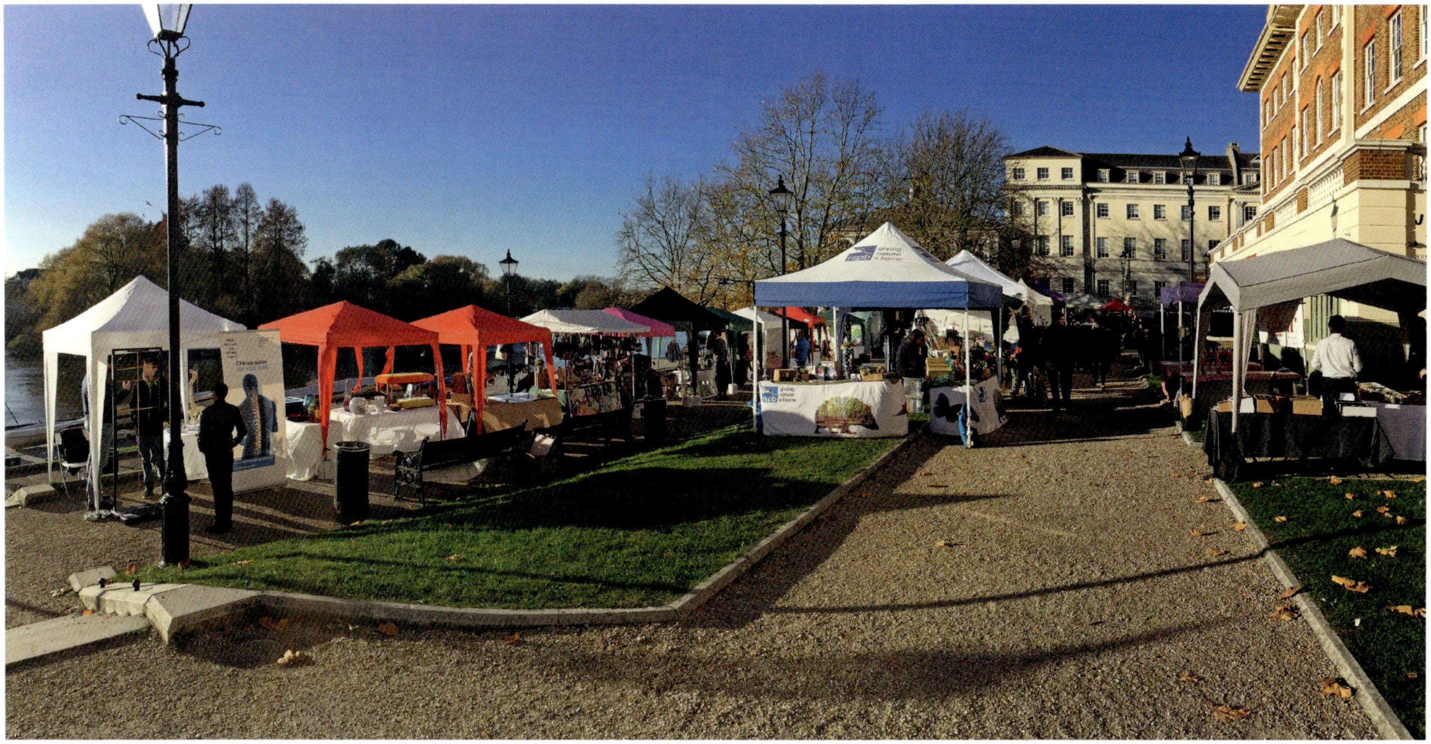

WWW.VISITRICHMOND.CO.UK
WWW.VISITRICHMOND.CO.UK

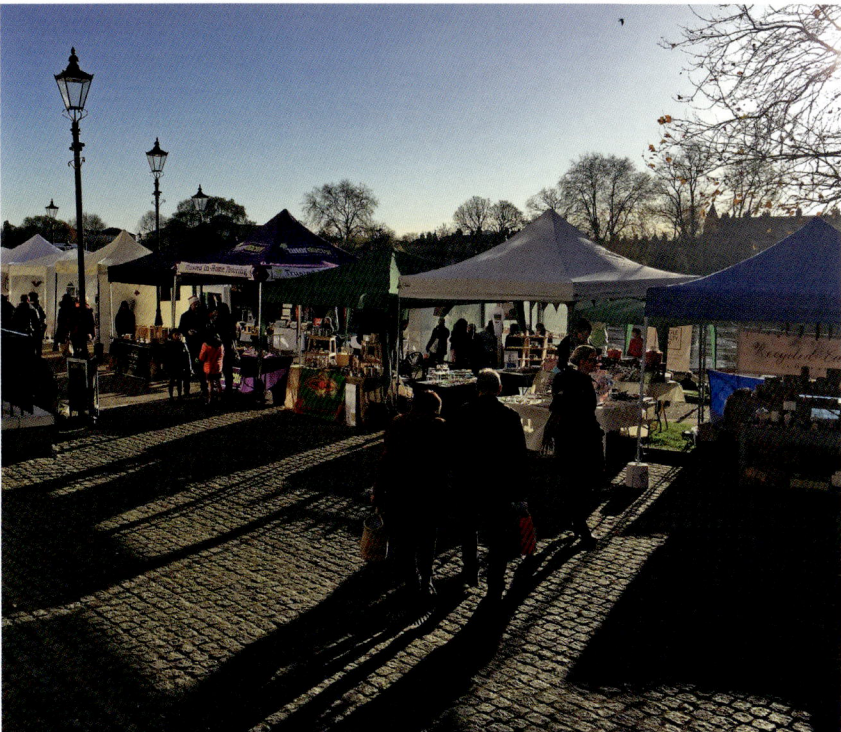

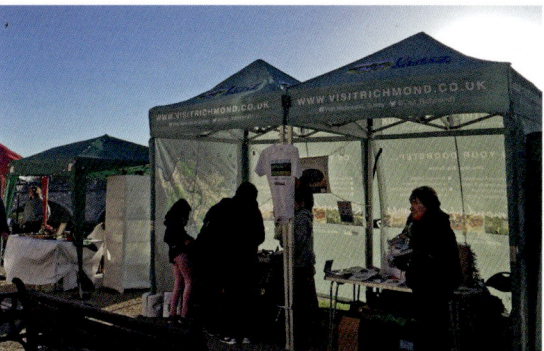

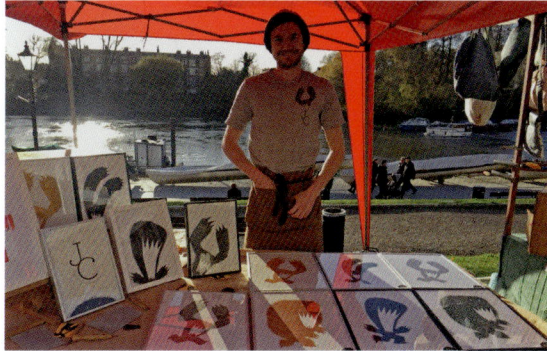

Above: Standing on the site where monks of the House of the Observant Friars worshipped in their chapel in the 16th century, the White Cross was originally known as the Waterman's Arms. By 1742 Samuel Cross was its proprietor, being succeeded by his sister-in-law Ann Cross and by the end of that century it was called by the current name. Rebuilt in the 1830s, it enjoyed a brief existence as a small hotel when cycling became a craze.

The Disappearing River

THE NOVEMBER DRAW-OFF

When London Bridge was rebuilt in 1832 the removal of the old palisades which acted as a weir resulted in the tides rising and falling far more quickly and often the river at Richmond was reduced to little more than a muddy stream and impassable to all but the smallest of crafts. After years of discussions as to how to resolve the problem, in 1894 a half tide lock and weir which also incorporated two footbridges was opened and so the river level was maintained upstream at Richmond. In November each year the weir is left open so that the river authorities can carry out any maintenance, hence the incredibly low tides.

The sun in the summer months slides directly into the river and can provide some glorious sunsets.

41

Turk Launches

This spread: The splendid vessels of Turk Launches, a 300-year-old company, are a familiar sight at St. Helena Pier. The New Southern Belle (main picture) has to lower its large black chimneys in order to get under the bridge. My wife even engaged them last year to entertain some of our friends to celebrate a rather large birthday I had and great fun it was.

Terrace Gardens

Below: The Coade stone statue of Old Father Thames – or the River God – cost the Duke of Montagu one hundred guineas when he bought it for the garden of his riverside house. After extending his grounds by purchasing the former kiln works, the tunnel grotto was built under Petersham Road to link his house with the river.

From Tudor times there had been tile kilns on the hillside between the river and Petersham Road where clay was dug out, but in 1776 the Duke of Montagu bought the land and added it to his own pleasure gardens. In turn his house was acquired by the Duke of Buccleuch who died in 1886, causing concern that the property would be bought by speculators and the area covered with villas, thus destroying the view. Sir John Whittaker Ellis purchased the house together with the former kiln ground for his own use and the Vestry bought the rest of the hillside land, thus creating the new Terrace Gardens. Fifty years later, the Vestry had become Richmond Council, who purchased and demolished Buccleuch House which reunited its land with the Terrace Gardens, though that part continues to be known as Buccleuch Gardens.

Overleaf: In the Gardens can be found a delightful little café, The Hollyhock (bottom left over page) which serves a delicious range of homemade cooked food.

The River Walk

TIME: APPROX. 1 HOUR

Start

Finish

1
2
3
4
5
6
7
8
9
10

On exiting Richmond station, cross the road and walk down narrow Old Station Passage, so named as it once led to the town's first railway station that opened in 1846, just south of where the present one stands. Turn left at Parkshot – a 'shott' in medieval times was a strip of land the length of a bowshot – and follow the path that cuts diagonally across Little Green (1). In Charles II's reign this was a bowling green whilst at the turn of the 20th century a Russian cannon captured in the Crimean War was displayed here. Continue along the path running across Richmond Green which must be one of the most beautiful greens in the country. In the Middle Ages it was the venue for jousting tournaments, cricket (2) has been played here since the 18th century and the annual May Fair continues to be the largest event organised in the borough. Maids of Honour Row on the river side, has graced the Green for over 300 years, they were built by Queen Caroline to house her ladies-in-waiting.

Continue into Old Palace Yard but before passing through the original Outer Gateway to the site of the former royal palace glance up at Henry VII's coat of arms carved in the stone work. To your left is the Wardrobe (3, 4 and 6) where furniture and soft furnishings would have been stored, whilst Trumpeters House ahead is so named because a stone figure of a trumpeter once stood each side of the house's entrance. Bear right and then left at Old Palace Lane. Just after the White Swan, a plaque (5) fixed to the wall records that Edward III, Henry VII and Elizabeth I all died at Richmond Palace. Asgill House, which stands on the site of the former brew house for the palace and is the only grand house remaining by the river's edge, was built around 1760 for Sir Charles Asgill, a Lord Mayor of London.

Turn left along Cholmondeley Walk which was constructed on reclaimed land and named after the Earl of Cholmondeley whose house was once here. Until the 18th century it was the only place in Richmond where you could walk by the river. The large heavily wooded island is a haven for herons and lies opposite the White Cross, where drinkers need to watch out for high tides otherwise they may require an impromptu boat ride back to dry land. A favourite place to sit and watch the river flow by is on the terraces of the new riverside development, where older listed buildings stand alongside new ones built in a variety of classical styles.

At the bridge, mount the steps to Bridge Street, originally called Ferry Hill, as it led to

the ferry which operated here until the bridge was built in 1776. Look upwards at the Italian style campanile of Tower House and across the road where a tall 18th century stone obelisk tells you the distances to various towns including Windsor. Ahead of you is the Art Deco influenced facade of the Odeon cinema. Turn left into Hill Street and on the corner of Whittaker Avenue, a splendid clock marks the passage of time outside the former Town Hall. The site was a gift to the town by Sir John Whittaker Ellis, a Lord Mayor of London who in turn became Mayor of Richmond.

Bear left into King Street which has been a popular location for taverns for many centuries; there has been a pub on this corner since 1692 and The Old Ship dates back to the 18th century. Pass number 8, which retains the old shop sign for J.H. Broad & Co. Ltd, turn right at number 19, which in 1893 was a family butcher, and this will take you into Paved Court, one of Richmond's many narrow alleyways. This leads to the Prince's Head. Originally known as the Duke of Ormonde's Head, it was

shortened to The Duke's Head after the Duke was exiled for treason and gained its current name when the Prince of Wales moved into the disgraced Duke's house. Before turning right into Golden Court (10) look across at the late 19th century stone drinking fountain (9) on Richmond Green which was restored to celebrate the Silver Jubilee of H.M. Queen Elizabeth II. Wander along Golden Court, formerly known as Pensioners Alley and lined with more independent shops, and into George Street, turning left to pass by the 1886 post office with its splendid coat of arms over the doorway. Mail gave way to retail nearly a century later. Courlander on the corner of Brewers Lane is the oldest jeweller in Richmond and has been in business since 1881. You will find more independent jewellers down this lane which leads you back to Richmond Green. Turn to your right and observe number 9, Onslow

House, where in 1801 George III visited George Onslow to tell him he was making him the first Earl of Onslow. Further along, the gothic house (7) was home to the Courlander family.

The theatre overlooking Little Green was designed by the renowned architect Frank Matcham in 1881, who gained the nickname 'Matchless Matcham', whereas the free public library next door had opened eighteen years earlier. Alongside the former Baptist Church there is narrow passage with a sign pointing to 'Richmond Library Annexe'. Follow it back to the busy main street. To the left, estate agents Chancellor have offices in a church like building but this is just how it looked when built by an earlier estate agent in 1884. Across the road is the 1930s Art Deco façade of the station and where the walk ends.

Walk devised by Caroline MacMillan
www.westlondonwalks.co.uk

East Twickenham

Main Picture:
Warren & Cambridge Gardens

Top right: The Pelabon's munitions factory (in Twickenham) was converted into Richmond ice rink and opened in 1928. It had the longest ice surface of any indoor rink in the world. It eventually closed in 1992, and luxury housing with views across the river to Richmond was built on the site.

This page: During the First World War, a community of around 6,000 Belgians settled in the area, many working in Charles Pelabon's munitions factory. They also established shops and businesses to serve their community whilst children attended a special 'Belgian Department' at Orleans School in St. Margarets. Thanks to a group led by Helen Baker (on the far right), on 1st April 2017 a special work of art was unveiled by the Belgian Ambassador, His Excellency Guy Trouveroy (second from right), as a memorial to this unique community of refugees who established a Belgian village on the Thames. Also pictured are The Mayor of Richmond David Linnette and far left, the grandson of Charles Pelabon.

Top left: The busy Richmond Road leading to the bridge. It links East Twickenham with Richmond.

Top right: Willoughby House, a 19th century villa, was formally known as Caen House and has a rather wonderful tower, which mirrors the one across the river beside the bridge.

Bottom left: Ryde House (known locally as Eagle House) was built around the same time as Willoughby House (opposite top), which together formed some of the first developments on Cambridge Park.

Opposite bottom left and right: Cambridge Gardens with its small café and tennis courts.

Street Scenes

Over the centuries Richmond has been a magnet for retailers and shoppers alike. The palace played an important part in this and the regular presence of the monarch and extensive retinue resulted in the opening of shops overlooking the Green, spreading up the alleyways and along George Street. Greengrocers, butchers and bakers traded alongside barbers and tailors, chandlers and farriers and the constant flow of visitors attending the Court ensured that ale houses and taverns were kept busy offering refreshment and overnight accommodation.

During the 19th century smaller shops began to give way to substantial stores and in 1877 Arthur and Frederick Wright established their emporium in George Street – Tesco Metro has taken its site – whilst J.H. Gosling opened his drapers shop even earlier in 1795 and successfully traded until eventually being acquired by the House of Fraser group. Whilst many of the earlier taverns have not stood the test of time, The Cricketers overlooking the Green has an unbroken history of serving ale since 1741, whilst the Old Ship on the corner of King and George Streets was open for business in 1766.

Today the busy streets of Richmond offer a wealth of variety to the local residents as well as the many visitors who travel to enjoy shopping in this unique town. George Street and The Quadrant have now attracted many major retail groups, whilst smaller King Street and Hill Rise still abound with independents. Major food chains have now arrived but tucked in the Courts are chocolateries and patisseries to tempt the hungry, as their predecessors would have done centuries before. Ale houses may have given way to wine bars and the Victorian post office become a dress boutique but Richmond continues to be the most delightful of towns in which to shop and then relax in one of its many cafés and restaurants.

Opposite: Golden Court – Originally Channon Row, by 1609 it was referred to as Pensioners Alley, probably due to pensioners passing down the passage on their way to the palace. It became Golden Court in 1905.

Richmond Green

Richmond Green is part of the Crown Estate and the 12 acres of open grassland is bordered by lime, plane and Norway maples and overlooked by many fine houses and historic buildings. It was the scene of many jousting tournaments during the Middle Ages and cricket has been played here since the 18th century.

Top right: Maids of Honour Row can be found on the south west side of The Green. The four elegant houses of Maids of Honour Row were built in 1724 to accommodate ladies-in-waiting to the then Princess of Wales. Although the first ladies were unmarried, they were addressed as Mrs as was the custom at the time and received £200 a year in addition to their board and lodging. Despite only being occupied by the Maids for a few years, the name remains.

A later resident of number 4 was Judith Levy, a very rich and eccentric Jewish widow who through her good works was known as the 'Queen of Richmond Green'. She paid most of the cost of rebuilding the Great Synagogue in Duke's Place, London, which her father had initially built at his own expense.

There are few reminders today of Henry VII's magnificent Palace of Richmond: The main gateway (top left), which bears his coat of arms, just off the south west side of the Green; Old Palace Yard (above); The Wardrobe, where soft furnishings were stored; and Trumpeters' House, which gained the name from two statues of trumpeting figures that once adorned the Middle Gate of the old Palace.

But when built, the palace was the showcase of the kingdom, the impressive frontage to the river with its many octagonal and round towers capped with pepper-dot domes, being typical of a 15th century castle. It contained the state apartments together with the king's private rooms which were linked to the Great Courtyard by a bridge across a moat. There were several courtyards around which were built a Great Hall, used for entertainment together with a substantial kitchen complex, a lavishly decorated chapel, under which lay the wine cellars, many rooms where officials and courtiers worked and slept, orchards and gardens. A side passage led to Crane Piece, a strip of open land stretching to the river where a crane unloaded goods and provisions brought by boat.

After the execution of Charles I the chapel, hall and private apartments were demolished and the stones sold and so by the Restoration of 1660, only the brick buildings and Middle Gate remained.

This page and overleaf: One fabulous Sunday in early April 2017, when the temperature reached 80 degrees and everyone flocked to the Green.

Previous page: The gracious white villas of Portland Terrace, with their fine view across the Green, are now listed buildings. Their name is a link to the Earl of Portland who assisted King Charles I in creating his new Great Park and was appointed its keeper, or ranger.

Top left: There had been no theatrical performances at Richmond since Queen Elizabeth's time but the New Theatre opened on Richmond Green in 1765 with the comic opera, *Love in a Village,* and the renowned actor Edmund Kean was theatre manager for the last two years of his life. This Georgian theatre was demolished in 1884 and Frank Matcham, the leading theatre architect of the day, was commissioned to design a new one overlooking Little Green which opened on the 18th September 1899 with a performance of Shakespeare's *As You Like It.*

Bottom left and right: Old Palace Terrace. In 1692 Virtue Radford employed local builder, William Wollins, to demolish an old mansion and replace it with a terrace of seven houses facing the Green and behind them a row of seven shops, those on the south-east side of Paved Court.

May Fair

Since 1971 the May Fair has taken place on the Green. It was originally conceived as a revival of a fair held in medieval times around the church of St. Mary Magdalene. Over the years it has grown in size and is now a popular annual family occasion with free entertainment all day including a funfair and more than a hundred stalls selling food and other items, many of which raise money for local charities.

Church Road and St Matthias Church

This spread: The 1857 church of St. Matthias was created as a chapel of ease for the expanding community and standing on the top of the hill, it is certainly the tallest church in Richmond. Designed by Sir George Gilbert Scott in Gothic revival style, the soaring spire reaching a height of 195 feet is a familiar landmark for miles around.

Top left: I rarely take pictures inside buildings but I made an exception for the church's wonderful rose window.

Bottom right: This was an unusual sight taken in the spring when Bishop's Pond in Richmond Park had dried up and some deer decided to investigate.

Friars Lane

This little lane bends its way past the site of former garden galleries of the old palace and also the outside wall of the monastery of Observant Franciscan Friars who lived here until 1534.

In 1581 Mr. Henry Harvey is recorded as having his 'mansion by the King's wall'. By 1749 it had been replaced by the Earl of Cholmondeley's larger house, which in turn became the property of the Earl of Queensberry. In 1934 this too was demolished and replaced by a private estate which retains the name of Queensberry House though some parts of the former houses were retained, including the magnificent cast-iron fountain which stands in the centre of the garden.

Friars Stile Road

Top left: The Vineyard School, which used to be in The Vineyard, hence its name but moved to its current site in the 1970s.

Top right: One of the first buildings on Friars Stile Road was Rose Cottage where Marie Gibbins ran a tea room. By the 1840s it had developed in to a hotel where novelist William Makepeace Thackeray often stayed, describing is as '*...one of the comfortablest, quietest, cheapest, neatest little inns in England...*'. Thirty years later Mrs Gibbins changed the name to The Marlborough and as a public house it survives to this day.

George Street

Right: A single storey Mechanics Institute was built in 1843 with an aim to provide adult education particularly in technical subjects. Twelve years later it had been converted into public baths which seems appropriate as this is where you would once have found the town's pond. An upper floor was added and over the years the building has served as Assembly Rooms, been a furniture store, cinema and contained numerous shops and offices. The dome added in 1908 gave the building, which is now listed, its name.

Left: J.H. Gosling founded his successful drapery store at 80 George Street back in 1795 and over the years it spread into several adjacent properties. The family firm was eventually acquired by the London department store of John Barker and is now part of the House of Fraser Group.

Bottom: The Open Book on King Street, just off George Street, celebrated its 35th anniversary in 2022.

Court Shopping

Several of the narrow shop-lined alleys which lead from George Street are known as courts and link busy George Street with the Green, where the monarch held court at the palace.

Opposite bottom left to right:
Church Court and Duke Street

This page: Paved Court – In 1814 the Vestry told the Surveyor of Highways that "a rail to be put at the end of Paved Alley next to the Green to prevent persons on Horse back going that way to the Town and that he do put down posts and turn stiles where necessary".

Opposite top: Brewers Lane – One of the oldest streets in Richmond, in the 17th century it was called Magpye Lane after the Magpye ale house which stood there but as more taverns opened in the lane, it so acquired the name of Brewers Lane.

Hill Street and Heron Square

Bottom left and opposite: Heron Square's name derives from Herring Court, created in the 1690s when a row of five houses along Hill Street and three mansions looking along the river were built on the site of the palace's former stables. A market is held here every weekend.

Bottom right: 2017 has seen the opening of a new restaurant in Hill Street, The Ivy, and despite all the disruption during its renovation I am glad to see that the famous vine has survived.

Opposite top: The rather fine tiling that can be found at the top of the Odeon building in Hill Street.

King's Road

Large villas started to line King's Road in the 1870s.

Former pupils of King's House School (bottom right) include local MP Zac Goldsmith and former England Rugby captain Lawrence Dallaglio.

Lancaster Park

The delightful terraces of Lancaster Park were built towards the end of the nineteenth century in the grounds of Lancaster House (bottom right).

Vine Row and Lancaster Passage date back many years and these charming cottages (bottom left) have escaped modern development.

Ancient Rights of Way

Richmond has many winding alleyways which follow the paths that once ran between fields. Originally used by agricultural workers, over the passage of time they have become public rights of way.

In 1696 Nathaniel Rawlins, a citizen and haberdasher, was fined 3s 4d for 'turning the Church way' when, in order to obtain a better forecourt to the mansion he had just built, he diverted a footpath leading to the church – the bend is still in Patten Alley though his house has long since gone.

Old Palace Lane

Below and opposite bottom: Just a few steps away from the river, the White Swan in Old Palace Lane dates back over two hundred years. Over time it has expanded into the adjoining cottage.

Hidden behind the gate in the wall in the picture (left) can be found the Old Palace Lane Allotments (top right and left and middle right). Built on land originally thought to be the Old Palace's moat, this is a magical little place, with 33 plots. You'd never know they were there and thank you to the committee, especially Anna Banham-Godfrey, for showing me around.

Paradise Road

Paradise Road is appropriately named as it leads worshippers to the Church of St. Mary Magdalene, where for more than 800 years they have heard of the paradise to come. Since 1953 it has also taken worshippers to the red brick First Church of Christ, Scientist (bottom left).

Opposite: The parish church dedicated to St. Mary Magdalene started life as a small chapel. It was considerably rebuilt during the late 1480s. In the early seventeenth century a new south aisle was added which was joined by one on the north side later the same century. Alterations and rebuilding work continued over the years, the last major change being the removal of the west gallery in the 1930s. The church contains some splendid monuments including one to Richard Fitzwilliam who founded the Fitzwilliam Museum and a flat stone outside marks the 1792 grave of John Lewis, the local campaigner to establish public rights of way across Richmond Park.

This page: The Odeon Studio Theatre opened in 1992 in a building that was previously a Mecca billiard hall. This modern entrance is a complete contrast to that of the Odeon 1930s Art Deco entrance just around the corner.

Park Road

THE HOLE IN THE WALL – THE RICHMOND MURDER MYSTERY

When Sir David Attenborough bought the derelict Hole in the Wall pub next door to his house in Park Road in 2010, his builders were somewhat surprised to unearth a skull buried under the former pub's stables. It was found to belong to Mrs. Thomas who had lived nearby and been murdered in 1879 by her maid, Kate Webster. She had dismembered the body, boiled up the fat to be sold as lard to unsuspecting neighbours and got them to help her carry heavy cases of 'rubbish' to the river at Richmond and Hammersmith, where they were subsequently thrown in. Kate went to the gallows with the secret as to what had happened to the head and it wasn't until 131 years later that the builders got the shock of their lives and the final part of poor Mrs. Thomas was finally laid to rest.

Petersham Road

Opposite top: The Bingham. Now a favourite riverside retreat and restaurant, there were originally two Georgian houses dating back to 1740 built here on the site of the Blue Anchor alehouse. When Lady Anne Bingham enlarged her house in 1820, the pub's malthouse was finally demolished and her mansion was duly enlarged.

Opposite bottom: My wife and some of our friends enjoying a charitable lunch at Chez Lindsay back in early 2017. Lindsay had kindly offered my friends their kitchen to cook food and the venue for the occasion.

Below: The British Legion Poppy Factory was founded in 1922 to give employment to wounded soldiers returning from the First World War. The workforce of five rapidly expanded and they outgrew their original premises in a former Bermondsey collar factory. The British Legion Poppy Factory, as it had become known, moved to the Lansdown Brewery site overlooking Petersham Road in 1925 where millions of poppies continue to be produced each year.

Prince's Road and the Alberts

The Alberts, a network of picturesque Victorian terraced cottages which provided homes for tradesmen, labourers, butchers, bakers and dustmen. This hidden area of Richmond acquired this name due to the ladder of streets running between Albert and Prince's Roads which were all named after members of the Queen's family – Albany, Lorne, Beatrice, York and Hyde.

In 1891 Jacob Neward was recorded as the beer retailer at The White Horse in Worple Way – 'worple way' is an old term for a bridle-path.

Bottom left: The former stables of the Aerated Water Manufacturing Company, which stood on the corner of Worple Way and Prince's Road in 1894, have now been converted to residential use.

Queen's Road

Bottom left: Standing near the top of Queen's Road and the Richmond Gate entrance to the park, The Lass O' Richmond Hill maintains the tradition that the lass referred to in the song was a local lady, although this is highly disputed by those who hail from Yorkshire.

Inset: Acting as a roundabout outside the Star and Garter is a decorative Art Nouveau style drinking fountain erected by the Royal Society for the Prevention of Cruelty to Animals and is one of the few remaining works by the notable Victorian architect T.E. Collcutt. As well as providing water for horses and cattle that toiled to the top of Richmond Hill, there is also a drinking trough for dogs at ground level.

There is another drinking fountain for people just to the right of the park gate: a granite column with two basins, which bears the inscription "H.R.H. Princess Mary Adelaide, Duchess of Teck, 27th October 1897".

Richmond Hill Open Gardens

Below top left and right and bottom left: Montague Road

Bottom right middle: Church Road

Bottom right: Dynevor Road

Opposite page inset and top left: Dynevor Road

Top right: Onslow Road

Bottom left, middle and right: Montague Road

Some of the other gardens can be found spread throughout the book in their respective sections – Rosemont Road on the next page, for instance.

Every other summer, some of the houses on the hill open up their gardens to the public and raise money for local good causes. The variety of gardens on show offer something for every garden lover: from the formal and ornate to natural and relaxed, city greenery and seasonal flowers, flourishing vegetables and herbs, complemented with interesting pergolas and water features. Sixteen houses participated in 2017, and four charities serving the local community were helped: INS (ins.org.uk) provides rehabilitation for people with long term neurological conditions such as Parkinson's disease, MS or strokes. Off The Record Twickenham (otrtwickenham.com) provides free and confidential counselling, information and a sexual health service to a thousand young people every year in Richmond borough. Richmond EAL Friendship Group (richmondeal.org. uk) offers free informal English lessons, advice and social activities to help speakers of English as an additional language overcome isolation. The Conservation Volunteers (tcv.org.uk/london/richmond) work in outdoor places across the UK to create healthier and happier communities. The Richmond Group offers volunteering experiences for local community members to get involved through practical conservation projects.

Rosemont Road & Gardens

Several of the houses on the east side of Rosemont Road (below top left) have exceptionally long gardens. This is the result of a parcel of land lying behind The Marlborough on Friars Stile Road being retained by the family when they sold the pub to the brewery. When the family's last descendant died in the 1950s this central strip of land was offered for sale to residents of Rosemont Road thus enabling several of them to increase the size of their gardens considerably, whilst also avoiding any possibility of it being built on.

Sheen Road

Opposite top right: The remains of the Temperance Permanent Building Society advertisement on the corner of Sheen Road. Formed in the 1830s, the company's directors supported the temperance movement and were required to sign The Pledge on a yearly basis.

Middle right: The Red Cow – starting life as an ale house in nearby Worple Way, the Red Cow tavern moved to its present site in 1789.

Bottom right: Beautiful wisteria covers the façade of Quinn's Hotel in spring.

Almshouses

Inset: Bishop Duppa's Almshouses in The Vineyard

Below and overleaf: William Hickey, Sheen Road

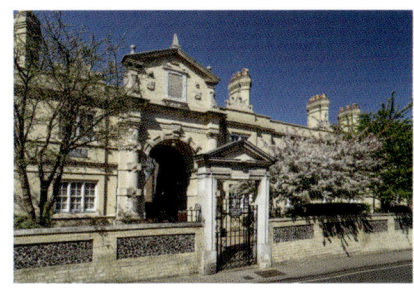

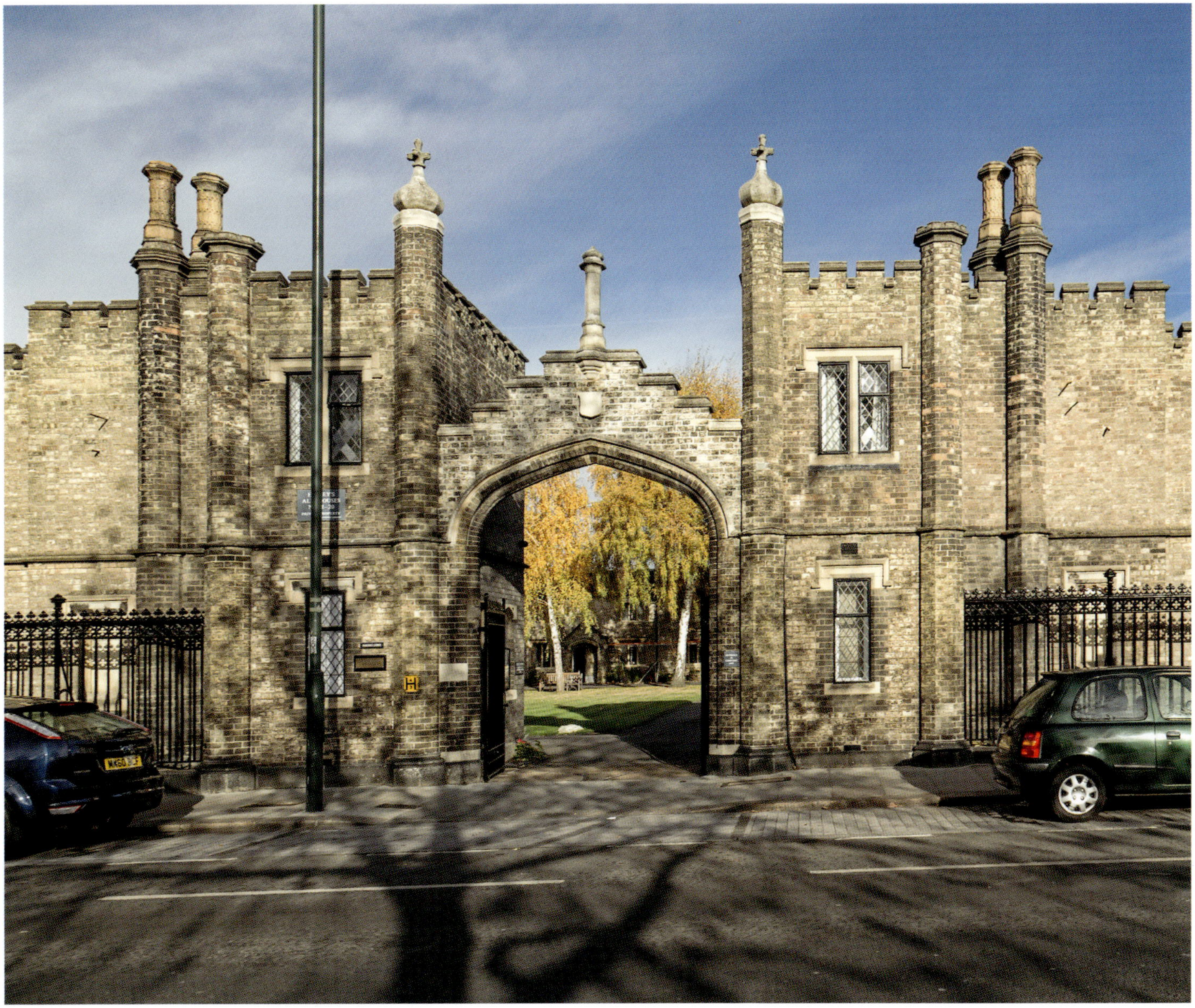

This and previous page: Almshouses – Many wealthy Richmond residents made bequests for the poor in their wills in the form of clothing, food or annual cash gifts, but the most generous were those who gave grants to endow almshouses. The first were founded for women in 1600 by Sir George Wright and built beside Petersham Road near today's Bridge Street, moving to their present site in The Vineyard in 1767, by which time they had adopted the name of Queen Elizabeth's Almshouses. Bishop Duppa's Almshouses, again for women only, were established in 1661 on Richmond Hill on the corner of Friar Stile Road and moved to their present Vineyard site some 200 years later. In 1695, ten houses for men, married or single, were given by Humphrey Michel and lay beside a lane leading to The Vineyard, after his death his nephew and heir, John Michel, increased the endowment. Rebecca and Susan Houblon, daughters of the first Governor of the Bank of England lived at Ellerker House on the Hill, now occupied by Old Vicarage School, and in 1769 would walk from their home along a green lane, today's Houblon Road, to the almshouses they founded for nine single women at Worple Way just off Sheen Road. These almshouse have never been rebuilt so remain the oldest ones still standing in Richmond.

Trustees of existing charities also founded almshouses in Richmond. When William Hickey died in 1727 he left provision to provide for the less fortunate and in 1834 his trustees appointed architect Lewis Vulliamy to build 20 almshouses facing Sheen Road (see previous page), ten each for men and women, together with a chapel and gate lodge houses for a porter and nurse. The Church Estate charity dates back to the reign of Queen Mary I and when they found themselves with an excess of funds in 1844, the trustees erected ten dwellings for both sexes adjoining those of the Hickey Almshouses. The newest almshouses in Richmond are those at Benn's Walk which are tucked away from the busy Kew Road roundabout and date from 1983.

The Quadrant

The Quadrant acquired the name in 1876 as it was the road which led to The Square. Earlier this part of Richmond was known as World's End, a common term given to the farthest house from a village centre.

Opposite: Richmond Station

Top right: The Railway Tavern

Bottom right: The Orange Tree Theatre was founded in 1971 as the Richmond Fringe in a small room above the Orange Tree pub, with just six former church pews providing the seating. Over the years the company has grown in reputation and size and now occupies its own spacious but still intimate theatre, with many more comfortable seats.

The Vineyard

The Vineyard follows the 15th century path between fields which led monks from their monastic home beside the palace to their vines growing on sunny slopes overlooking the river.

Top left: The Dukes Head Inn – in 1881, Harry Alexander was the publican and lived there with his brother, sister-in-law and one servant.

Below: The Roman Catholic St Elizabeth of Portugal Church, with its splendid green dome and spire, is dedicated to the beautiful fourteenth century wife of King Denis of Portugal. As well as attending mass every day, she was a model of kindness towards the poor and a successful peacemaker between members of her own family as well as nations.

Richmond at Christmas

Bottom right: Fortunately the rain held off when Richmond officially turned on its illuminations in late November 2016. In attendance were The Mayor, actors Maureen Lipman and Chris Jarvis, and Scott Brown from the sponsors, London Square. Master of ceremonies and chief singer for the evening was my friend Shelle Luscombe (far right).

A walk around the town

Map © OpenStreetMap.org contributors

This walk around Richmond begins at the railway station, a splendid 1930s Art Deco building. Turn left along The Quadrant, the part of town which in the 17th century was known as World's End, a common term given to the farthest house or field from a village centre. Take a short detour by turning left into pedestrianised Waterloo Place (1) with its terrace of delightful cottages which emerges alongside the red brick fire station (2) – it replaced an old fire watch-house and when built in 1870 also provided accommodation for the stand-by firemen. Bear right, glancing up at three stern carved faces looking down from the old fire station (2), the two either side of Father Thames wearing a Victorian fireman's helmet. Go left into the busy George Street and at Tesco turn left into Church Court. The Angel and Crown has been serving drinks since the early eighteenth century but the church of St. Mary Magdalene (3) has been here for more than 800 years. Bear left and behind the wall of number 6 are the charming old Parish Church Rooms. Continue up Church Walk to Paradise Road and turn left. Look down at St. James's Cottages (4) as you pass by and also across the road to The Vestry House, its name being a reminder that in the 18th century the town's Vestry Hall was located in this road, the vestry being the predecessor of the local council. Further along a blue plaque records that Leonard and Virginia Woolf (5) lived in this house for nine years and it is where they founded their printing press.

Ahead is the red brick First Church of Christ Scientist but cross the road and turn into Mount Ararat Road. In the 1740s a large country house stood further up the hill and Mount Ararat was a popular name around that time for houses standing on rising

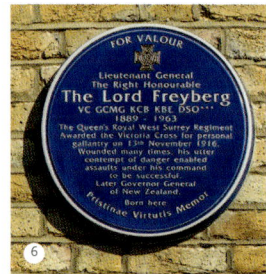

ground. By 1825 its lodge house had become a boys' school and was described by a former pupil as 'a wretched sham-Gothic schoolroom built, I believe, with a special view to keeping the boys in a freezing condition during the winter'. Turn left into Dynevor Road built on land owned by the Selwyn family and so named as one of the daughters married the 2nd Baron Dynevor in 1794. A blue plaque at number 8 marks the birthplace of Bernard Freyberg (6), a soldier who distinguished himself in the First World War by winning a VC and in the Second being called 'The Salamander' by Churchill for his desire to be in the middle of the action and astonishing ability to survive.

At Church Street turn right, take the first left into Preston Place and descend the steps at the end into Houblon Road. When it was a lane in 1757, surrounded by fields, Rebecca and Susanna Houblon walked down it from their house on Richmond Hill to visit the almshouses they founded close to Sheen Road. Go right into Albany Passage, right at the next alleyway and first left into another little alleyway to reach Albert Road; these streets of picturesque terraced cottages are collectively called 'The Alberts' as several are named after members of Queen Victoria's family. Turn right and then bear left into Audley Road. The small row of Maxwell Cottages (7) is a reminder that Mr. John Maxwell, a Victorian publisher and husband of the then popular novelist Mary Braddon, built houses in this area in the 1860s and named this road after one of her best-known books: Lady Audley's Secret. Turn right at King's Road which retains many of the original Victorian villas built in the mid-19th century when fields finally gave way to bricks and mortar. At the junction with Marchmont Road – another road bearing the name of a Mary Braddon novel – turn right into what appears to be a cul-de-sac but where at the far end you will be find Albany Passage leading off the right, originally a footpath running along the edge of the fields. Proceed slowly and turn left into an unmarked alleyway opposite the third lamp post which will take you back to the top of Houblon Road and the steps to return you to Preston Place.

Cross Church Road and enter The Vineyard which, as the name indicates, was where the monks would have grown their vines until the dissolution of the monasteries.

The former British School (9) opened in 1867 and when air raid shelters were built in the 1940s, the builders found an old well and a wine-press. Opposite were the original stables for Mount Ararat House (8), which by 1919 were being used by entrepreneur Joseph Mears, who co-founded Chelsea Football Club, as garages for the motor coaches he hired out for private outings. One of the drivers lived in the house in the middle.

Follow The Vineyard as it bears to the right to reach Queen Elizabeth's Almshouses which were founded in 1600 though today's buildings replace those damaged in the last war. Next door are those established by Bishop Duppa in 1661 and rebuilt here nearly two hundred years later though the impressive gateway comes from the original site. Just a few paces away are Michel's Almshouses which were built on this site in 1696 and rebuilt at the turn of the 19th century. Set back from the road is delightful Clarence House, so named as the Duke of Clarence is alleged to have slept here. Bernardo O'Higgins (10), one of Chile's founding fathers, lived here for a short while as did Brian Blessed who owned the house in the 1970s.

The Roman Catholic Church of St. Elizabeth of Portugal was designed by Thomas Hardwick and dates from 1824, whereas the Congregational Church next door was built some seven years later. On reaching Hill Rise turn right but pause outside number 84 to admire the wonderful tiles which date from when it was a dairy for Hornby and Clarke whose cows grazed on nearby Petersham Meadows. Pass by The Victoria Inn with its pint-sized bar and turn right by the cinema into Ormond Road (11) with its delightful terrace of Georgian houses. Opposite the Unitarian Church are The Rosary and The Hollies (12), a pair of houses built back-to-back by Nathaniel Rawlins (who also built Clarence House) for his two daughters who, in the event, never lived in them.

Turn left at The Hermitage into Church Terrace (13). The Bethlehem Chapel was built in 1797 by John Chapman, a market gardener from Petersham. Cross the main road by the former forge which during World War II was used for storing ammunition and enter the old burial ground of St. Mary Magdalene. To the left of the church's west door is the tomb of William Hickey whose almshouses overlook Sheen Road. Follow round the church, turn left into Church Court and at George Street turn right, where overlooking The Square is the Dome Building which during its life time has been a library, public baths, assembly rooms and a cinema. Continue along The Quadrant past the Railway Tavern which in 1855 offered rooms to those who had missed their last train and your walk ends where it began, at the railway station.
Walk devised by Caroline MacMillan
www.westlondonwalks.co.uk

Richmond Cemetery

AND PESTHOUSE COMMON

The cemetery on Lower Grove Road opened in 1786 in a rural area and since then has expanded several times. Two Gothic revival style chapels were built in the 19th century, one for Anglicans and the other for Nonconformists. Sir Edwin Lutyens designed the memorial dedicated to the 39 soldiers who died at the South African Hospital in Richmond Park during the First World War and there is a special section for departed residents of the Royal Star and Garter Home. Felix Pissarro, the 23 year old son of Impressionist painter Camille, also rests here. He died of TB in a sanatorium in Kew Road in 1897.

Bottom right: There were pest houses on the fringes of many villages and towns where those suffering from the plague or other infectious ailments were sent until they either recovered or died – an early form of quarantine. Richmond's stood on common land well away from the town and a small open area is still called Pesthouse Common. The pest house itself was pulled down when a new workhouse and burial ground was built nearby just off Queen's Road in 1787.

Clockwise from top left: Small Copper, Common Blue, Painted Lady and a Mother Shipton Moth.

In the spring, there was a wonderful show of daisies in the cemetery, which attracted a fabulous array of butterflies. Sadly, before the daisies had finished flowering, the council's contractor cut them all down. I realise that they have a duty of care towards the upkeep of the grounds but surely most people wouldn't object if nature was allowed to flourish at certain times of the year.

Opposite centre: Standing at the top of Richmond Hill is a delightful terrace of houses which also incorporate the Roebuck. Number three, a Georgian house with Palladian influences, was designed by Sir Robert Taylor who was also responsible for the ceremonial coach used annually at the Lord Mayor's Show. Mrs Fitzherbert lived here and after undergoing a form of marriage to the Prince of Wales, later King George IV, it is allegedly where they spent their honeymoon.

Opposite top: The Wick and Wick House – As owner of St. Michael's Mount in Cornwall, Lady St. Aubyn would not have been worried by winds howling up the hillside from the Thames when she had the Bull's Head tavern demolished in 1775 and built The Wick. In more recent years this elegant villa has been home to Sir John Mills and his family as well as several members of the Rolling Stones, the latter who used Wick Cottage just down Nightingale Lane as a party house.

Sir Joshua Reynolds so loved the view from Richmond Hill that in 1772 he commissioned Sir William Chambers to build Wick House for him where he lived until his death twenty years later. By the late 1940s it provided accommodation to nurses from the adjacent Star and Garter Home.

Opposite bottom left: In 1620, the Grist Wind Mill overlooked the town below and for a hundred years ground the inhabitants' corn. It was where the Richmond Gate Hotel is today.

The Petersham

HOTEL & RESTAURANT

The Petersham has undergone many changes both in name and structure since Nightingale Cottage stood here in 1770, when the sweet song of that bird could be heard on Richmond Hill. The cottage was rebuilt and became Ashburnham Lodge in 1865 and that in turn was replaced by the Italian gothic style Richmond Hill Hotel which some 30 years later was called The Mansion Hotel. When the famous old Star and Garter Hotel was demolished, the hotel called itself the New Star and Garter, but it was all change again in 1945 when the Bank of England acquired the property for staff accommodation and they knew it as Nightingale Hall. Six years later it reverted back to being the Star and Garter Hotel but the final change was when it acquired new owners in 1978 who named it The Petersham Hotel. One thing has remained constant over the centuries and that is the spectacular view across Petersham Meadows to the Thames, glistening in the valley below.

Petersham

Petersham's history dates back to the seventh century when the meadows of Piterichesham – Anglo Saxon meaning 'the home of Patricius' – belonged to Chertsey's Benedictine Abbey, eventually coming to the Dysart family who were Lords of the Manor ten centuries later. The rural aspect attracted many aristocrats, such as the Duke of Argyll who commissioned James Gibbs to build Sudbrook House, which remains a superb example of his Palladian style. The Dowager Duchess of Montrose gave her name to Montrose House, as did the Duchess of Rutland who resided in neighbouring Rutland Lodge. The railway did not reach Petersham so the village escaped intensive Victorian development, though it had a narrow escape when Mrs Warde bought the Earl of Bute's house and grounds in 1894. After demolishing the house she intended to create a new residential suburb but died before her plans could be put into action and only All Saints' Church and adjoining hall remain as a monument to her dreams. During World War II the village was requisitioned by the Anti-Aircraft Command and as All Saints' had never been consecrated, the campanile was used as a RADAR training centre.

Lying in the curve of the Thames it is not surprising that with its network of ancient footpaths and alleyways linking roads, the ancient church of St. Peter, notable houses and open spaces, that Petersham was once reputed to be the most elegant village in England. For centuries cows have grazed the riverside meadows and a parliamentary act passed in 1902 safeguarded this open land, in doing so preserving the famous view from Richmond Hill for prosperity.

It is always a joy to see the distinctively marked Belted Galloways grazing on Petersham Meadow. Affectionately known as the 'Beltie', they are beef cattle originating from Galloway in south west Scotland and a familiar sight to walkers from spring to the autumn – they take a winter holiday elsewhere.

136

Standing proud on top of Richmond Hill, the Star & Garter started life in 1738 as a modest tavern. It expanded over the years although the ballroom and dining room, added at the turn of the nineteenth century, bankrupted its owner. Re-opened by Christopher Crean, a former chef to the Duke of York, it continued to flourish: crowned heads of Europe stayed, Queen Victoria visited and banquets entertained the great and the good including a former President of the United States. During the 1860s, the oldest buildings were replaced by one designed in French chateau style and following a fire in 1870, the hotel gained a pavilion with a dining room seating 250. London's Society flocked to Richmond to enjoy a day in the countryside and dine at the Star & Garter. But with the arrival of motorised transport it was possible to travel further afield and the hotel's fortunes declined and in 1907 it was put up for sale. In 1915, the site was bought by public subscription and presented to Queen Mary but as the existing buildings were not suitable for hospital use, it was rebuilt to a design by Sir Edwin Cooper and finally opened as the Royal Star & Garter Home for Disabled Sailors, Soldiers and Airmen in 1924.

More recently, the Star & Garter Home has moved to a purpose built residence in Surbiton. The old building has been turned into luxury apartments by London Square.

By the turn of the 20th century there was great public concern that Petersham Meadows, which for several centuries had been part of Ham House estate, could be built on but an Act of Parliament passed in 1902 ensured protection of the view from Richmond Hill. The tenancy of Petersham Farm has been passed down over the years and grazing cows have become a familiar sight on the Meadows.

Petersham Nurseries

Opposite: Rutland Lodge, beyond Petersham House (main picture opposite) was orginally built in 1660 for Sir William Bolton who became Lord Mayor of London. When he was unable to account for £1,800 from collections made for those who suffered in the Great Fire of London, he was forced to resign from public duties and eventually was so poor the Court of Common Council voted him a pension of £3 a week.

Petersham House dates back to 1680 and is now famous for the Nurseries which were created out of the grounds in the 1970s.

Petersham Road

Bottom right: The Arts and Crafts building for *The Dysart* dates back to 1904 although there has been a pub on the site for several centuries. The name refers to the Earls of Dysart who were lords of the manors of Ham and Petersham for over three centuries. The oak bar is believed to come from a decommissioned warship from Napoleonic times.

Top right: *The Fox and Duck*, formerly the *Horse and Groom*, was completely rebuilt in the '40s but the original white painted watchman's lock-up and village pound, situated alongside it, remains as it is a listed building. In 1787 the watchman received eleven shillings a week to guard the village from 9pm until 3am.

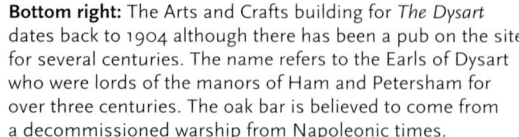

Opposite top left: Although it looks very old, the gatehouse to Ham House only dates from 1900 and was designed for the Dysart family in a Jacobean style. It leads to Douglas House (opposite bottom left), an early 18th century Queen Anne style house which has housed the German School since the mid-'70s and Ham Polo Club (opposite middle right).

This page: There has been a church on this site since Saxon times and an entry in the Domesday Book suggests that it had by then already undergone some restoration. A new Norman church was built in 1266 but little of this remains due to the rebuilding of the main body of the church in the early sixteenth century, whilst a century later the north and south transepts were added together with the tower. The church is one of the few to retain box pews and galleries which were installed in 1840.

It is reputed that Prince Rupert of the Rhine, a cousin of Charles II, married Lady Francesca Bard, the mother of his son, in the church but the parish registers are incomplete so this cannot be proved. A more recent marriage with royal connections took place in 1881 when the future Earl of Strathmore married Nina Cavendish-Bentinck – their youngest daughter, Elizabeth, became Queen of England in 1936.

The quiet churchyard contains the tombs of many notable people who have lived in Petersham over the centuries including Mary Burdekin, believed to have been the first baker of the Maids of Honour pastries and the maritime explorer George Vancouver, who sailed with Captain Cook and after whom Vancouver Island is named.

Sudbrook Lane

This spread: The Sudbrook, or 'south brook' rises in Richmond Park and flows downwards to join the Thames. Until put underground, it ran alongside the main Petersham Road and was crossed by a ford at the junction of Sudbrook Lane. When the culvert collapsed in the 1970s, it was referred to as the Petersham Hole and caused traffic disruption for more than a year.

Opposite bottom right: Bute House was just one of the many mansions owned by the Earl of Bute who served as Prime Minister under King George III. The estate was bought at the end of the nineteenth century by Mrs Lionel Warde, who planned a suburban development, but after commissioning the building of the red brick Italian Romanesque basilica of All Saints' Church and adjacent hall, she died. The church has never been consecrated and is now a private residence, but at one time it was used as a recording studio and Luciano Pavarotti recorded his best-selling album 'O Holy Night' here.

This Page: The Old Vicarage with All Saints Church in the background.

Richmond Golf Club

This spread: Designed by James Gibbs in splendid Palladian style for the 2nd Duke of Argyll who was born nearby at Ham House, Sudbrook Park was handed down through the family until 1819 when it was eventually sold. The park has been home to the Richmond Golf Club for over 100 years, the Grade I listed house serving as their clubhouse. I was extremely grateful to the player finishing up his round that he just stayed in the light, as otherwise I might have been obliged to ask him to take it again.

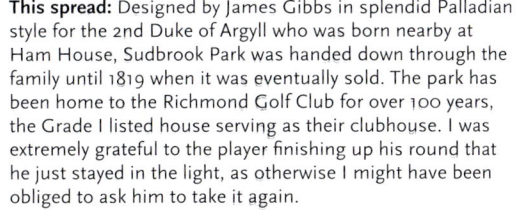

Old Deer Park

When Charles I created his new Great Park, the remaining hunting fields lying between Richmond town and Kew adopted the name of Old Deer Park. The arrival of the railway cutting across one corner and then construction of the new arterial road to Chertsey, has heightened its feeling of separation from the town. It is certainly a 'keep fit' park as the course and club house of the Mid-Surrey Golf Club has been here since 1892, the Richmond Athletic Ground is housed here and it has for many years been home to the London Welsh Rugby Football Club.

For over seventy years a horse show took place annually at Old Deer Park. It began when a local vet was impressed by the quality of the horses and carriages bringing spectators to a cricket match on the Green. The impressive and popular show ran over three days and was often attended by members of the Royal Family but eventually lack of space to accommodate further expansion saw the last one being held in 1967.

THE RICHMOND HORSE SHOW: A GENERAL VIEW OF THE DRIVING MARATHON, WHICH IS ONE OF THE MOST SPECTACULAR EVENTS.

The Richmond Royal Horse Show opened in the Old Deer Park at Richmond on June 9, and the three-day programme was favoured throughout by brilliant weather. The Driving Marathon, open to pairs, was one of the features of the first day. It was won by Mr. H. J. Colebrook, who showed a finely matched pair of bays driven by Miss Colebrook, who is aged fourteen. It was later announced that the Queen would offer a special cup at next year's show.

A clipping from a local paper covering The Royal Horse Show from 1932

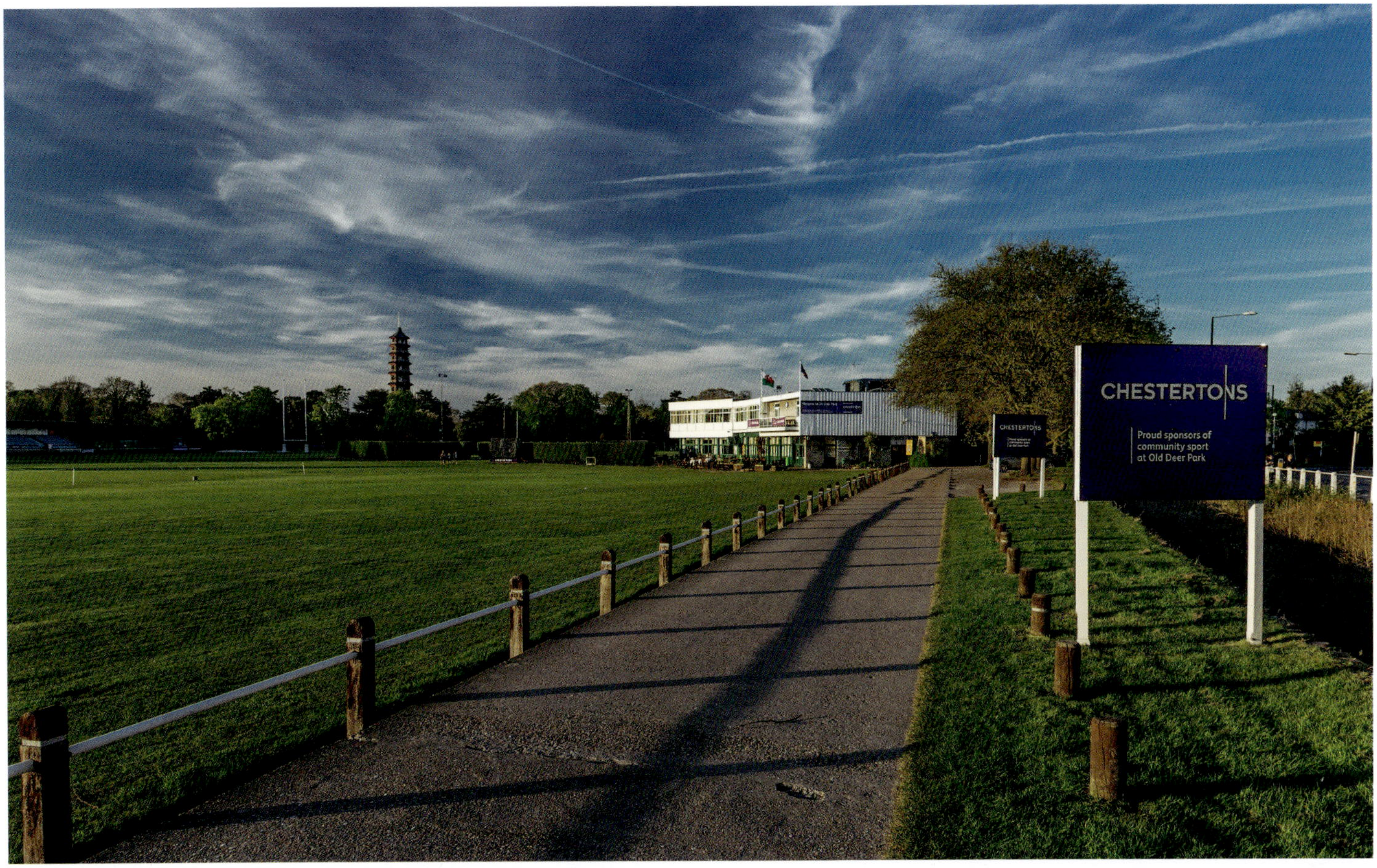
CHESTERTONS
Proud sponsors of
community sport
at Old Deer Park

CHESTERTONS

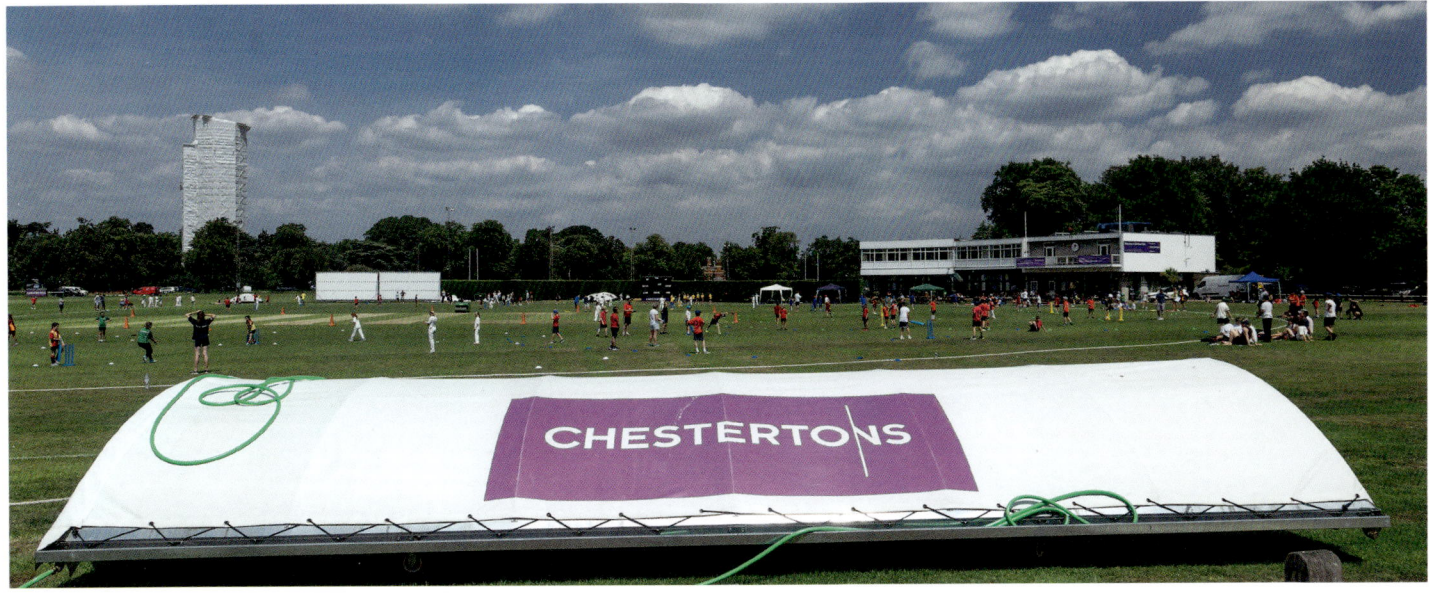

Richmond footbridge, weir and lock as viewed from Twickenham Bridge

Royal Mid-Surrey Golf Club

Founded on October 24th 1892 – St. Crispin's Day – the Royal Mid-Surrey Golf Club is so named as it lies on the edge of the counties of Middlesex and Surrey, acquiring royal status when the Prince of Wales became Captain in 1926. The magnificent two 18-hole courses lie on Crown Estate land whilst the modern club house replaces one that was burnt to the ground in just 45 minutes in 2001.

Bottom left: Sitting in the middle of Old Deer Park is The King's Observatory. George III was fascinated with the science of his day and commissioned William Chambers to construct an observatory in his park in order to view the passage of Venus across the sun on the 3rd June 1769, something which happens only once in 245 years. Three obelisks were erected in the park to assist in the exact alignment

of instruments in the King's Observatory before the task was transferred to the one at Greenwich. He was also interested in time-keeping and possessed an accurate clock made by Benjamin Vulliamy which was used to provide a standard time to important London government buildings.

Kew

Standing in stately splendour, St. Anne's Church dominates Kew Green. Until the early eighteenth century local residents were compelled to travel five miles along muddy tracks to attend church in Kingston. In 1714 a group of Kew landowners decided it was time they had their own place of worship and agreed to meet the cost of the small and plain chapel erected on Kew Green; their individual contributions were mostly around the £10 mark whilst Lady Capel gave a generous £50. When it appeared that the estimated building cost of £250 would be double that amount she donated a further £50, however there was still a shortage and she headed the list of subscribers who eventually covered the entire debt.

Mr. Thomas Fogg was the first curate of St. Anne's but by 1717 he was upsetting his parishioners who wrote to the bishop listing his many faults which included him retaining the collections rather than giving the money to the poor, ringing the church bell for barely 15 minutes rather than 30 which meant many were late arriving for the service and, worst of all, wearing boots and riding clothes under his surplice. The bishop wrote firmly to Mr. Fogg ordering him to mend his ways which he must have done as no more complaints were received from the disgruntled flock, though it is not known what he continued to wear under his surplice.

St Anne's Church, 1850

Kew Green

This spread: The Green originally had no fence but grazing cattle caused problems and in 1824 a sturdy wooden fence was installed, eventually to be replaced by iron railings which were given as scrap in the Second World War, apart from the ones round the little triangle outside the Garden's main gate.

A honeycomb of air-raid shelters in the Green offered safety during the Blitz whilst the 'Dig for Victory' campaign saw allotments on the surface – apart from the hallowed cricket square.

A fair was regularly held on the Green but suppressed in 1781 due 'to nuisances'. Last century, a popular Easter Monday Fair attracted the crowds but it was not revived after World War II.

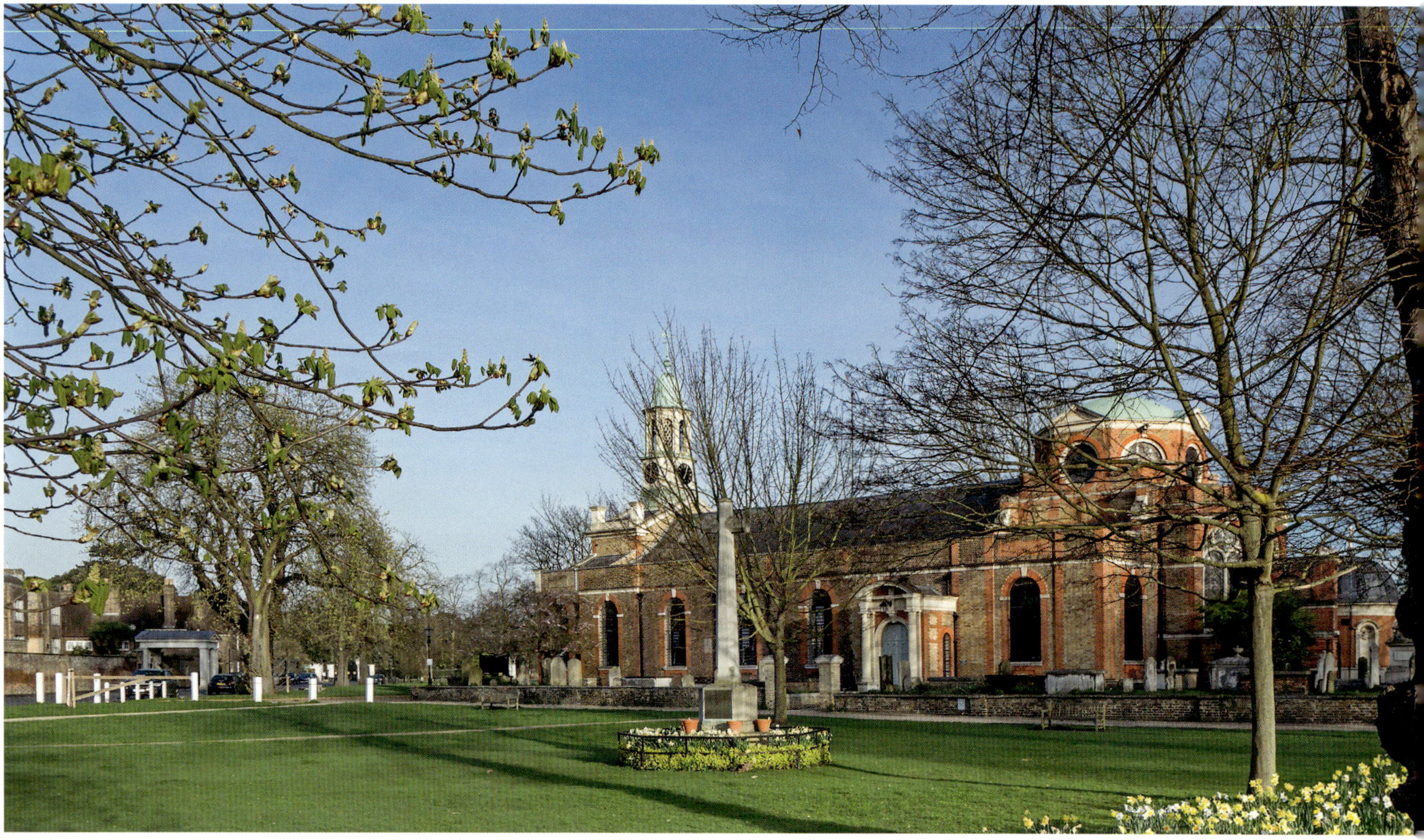

THE PARISH CHURCH OF ST ANNE, KEW GREEN

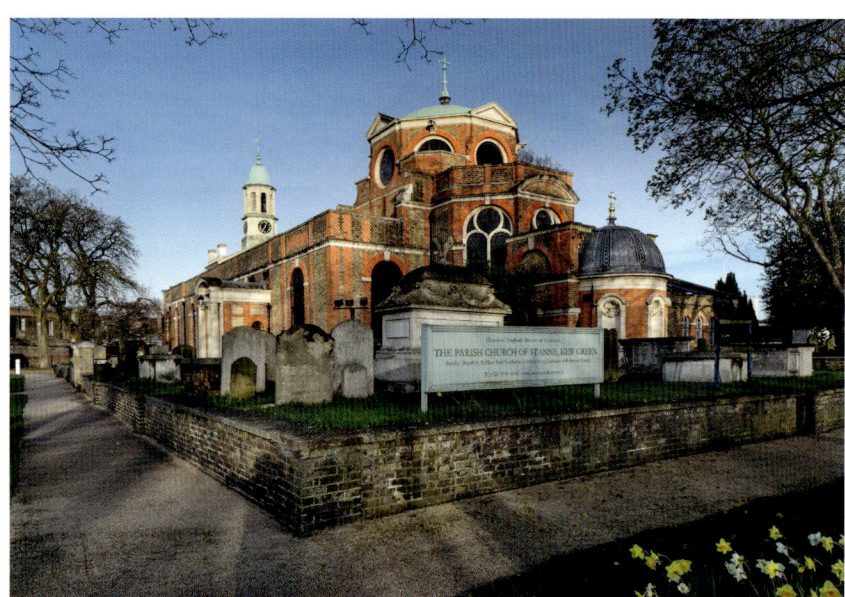

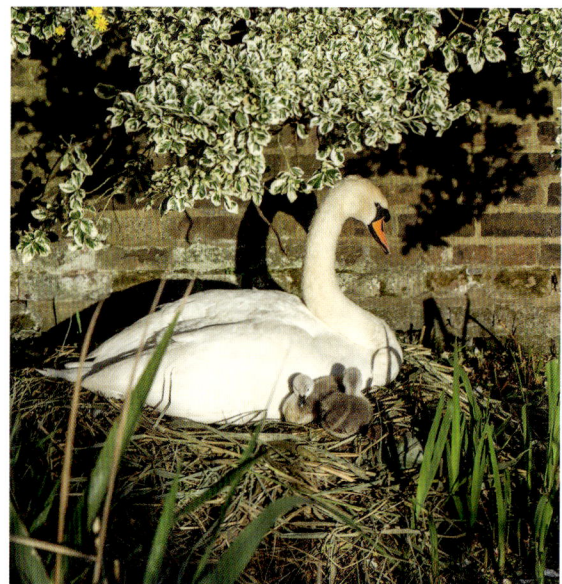

Bottom left: Amongst the many graves found in the church yard, is that of Thomas Gainsborough, one of Great Britain's finest painters.

Bottom right: the entrance to Kew Green Preparatory School

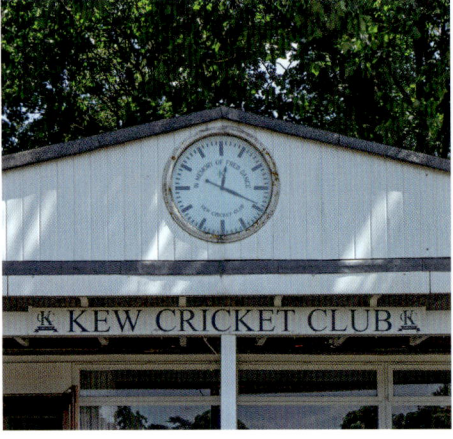

Kew Midsummer Fête

Starting in its current form in 2010, the fête is entirely run by volunteers and has raised many thousands of pounds for local good causes.

Kew Bridge and the River

The first wooden bridge connecting Kew with Brentford was not a success and at one point it was forced to close for a couple of years following a collision. 1789 saw the opening of an elegant stone one with George III leading 'a great concourse of carriages' across it and it remained a toll bridge until 1873, with foot passengers paying one halfpenny and horses sixpence. With the increase in traffic it was necessary to widen the road and it was completely rebuilt in 1903. It is still possible to see shrapnel marks on the sides of the bridge which are the result of a bomb which fell nearby on the evening of 24th February 1944.

OLIVER'S ISLAND

Oliver's Island, or *Ait* as these Thames river islands are known, lies between Kew's railway and road bridges. Legend has it that Oliver Cromwell escaped to it via an underground tunnel from the Bull's Head on the north bank where he had established his headquarters, but no tunnel has ever been found and no documents of that era confirm this tale. Now thickly wooded it is a haven for cormorants, herons, Canada geese and ducks.

Now and then: The view of Kew Bridge from Strand on the Green, today and from the 1800s.

The new developments on the far side of river have radically changed the way this area now looks.

Inset opposite: Pictures from 2010, before the completion of the latest developments.

Above: Kew Pier is a popular stopping place for tourists enjoying river trips from Westminster to Hampton Court.

This page: The modern residential development of Kew Riverside.

Kew Road & Kew Foot Road

Top left: Kew Road. Now a Tesco, the classic Art Deco frontage of the Matthiae's Café & Bakery remains. For more than 80 years the family's bakery and catering department was on the ground floor, a café and banquet on the first and a ballroom, also in Art Deco style, on the top floor.

Below middle: Kew Foot Road was once known as Love Lane. The terrace of three Georgian houses to the left of The Triple Crown (which was The Tulip Tree back in 1884) have some wonderful carved door heads (opposite inset left).

This page: When the subscription dinner of 1863, given on Richmond Green for schoolchildren and the poor to celebrate the marriage of the Prince of Wales, resulted in a surplus of £40, it was decided to use this sum to build a small hospital. An appeal was launched which raised sufficient funds to purchase Rosedale in Kew Foot Road, former home to the poet James Thomson who had penned the lyrics to 'Rule Britannia'. The Richmond Infirmary opened in 1868 and when Queen Victoria became Patron some twenty-seven years later, it was re-named Royal Hospital, Richmond. The wards closed in 1977 but the hospital continues as a psychiatric day hospital and mental health resource centre.

This page: Tradition has it that Henry VIII so enjoyed the taste of a dainty tart being served to Anne Boleyn and her Maids of Honour at Richmond Palace, that he demanded the recipe be kept secret from all except the baker. From the early 18th century these melt-in-the-mouth pastries could be purchased from a shop in Richmond, where a young Robert Newens served his apprenticeship. He in turn handed the secret recipe on to his son Alfred who opened a new establishment in Kew Road in 1850, where it remains to this day.

Page opposite: The 1930s mansion block estate of Gloucester Court, off Kew Road, stands on the site of Gloucester House, the summer residence for one of George III's brothers. From 1840 until the First World War it became Mr and Mrs Neumegen's private boarding school for Jewish children.

Sandycombe Road

Until 1884 Sandycombe Road was known to local residents as Sandy Lane, prior to that as Blind Lane.

Lawn Cresent

The attractive crescent of houses of Lawn Crescent overlooking a central open green were built around 1900 and formed part of the suburban development of Kew.

Number 26 was once home to Helena Swanwick, a dedicated suffragist and sister to the painter Walter Sickert.

Station Parade

One of the first businesses established when Kew station opened in 1869 was the estate agent, Breadmore and Webb, who remained there for 100 years, their office is now the Kew Bookshop.

At the turn of the 20th century, Josiah Clarke and Sons had established a dairy and creamery at 7 Station Parade. It is currently a Starbucks coffee shop.

Right, second from top: This new bench at the corner of the parade and Sandycombe Lane is dedicated to a lovely local man, David Blomfield, who sadly passed away in 2016. I hadn't known David long but in the brief time we knew each other he helped me greatly with my original book on Kew and passed on much of what he knew about writing and publishing; advice I have put to good use this past five years as I have continued to add to my series of books on the villages of South West London.

Right, second from bottom: When Kew Station opened on 1 January 1869, it lay amidst orchards and market gardens. The delightful yellow brick station buildings are fine examples of Victorian railway architecture and together with the footbridge are Grade II listed. It is also the only station on London Underground with a pub attached to a platform. Once simply known as *The Railway*, when the *Tap on the Line* first opened, there was a door from the pub which could access the station platform.

Pagoda Avenue

The Selwyn family owned extensive market garden land in Kew and Richmond and their family home was called Pagoda House. Selwyn and Pagoda Avenues lie where it formerly stood.

Ennerdale Road

Built on the former Selwyn estate in the 1800s, Ennerdale Road follows the medieval boundary line between fields.

The National Archives

Until the passing of the Public Record Office Act in 1838 to 'keep safely the public records', they were located diversely at Westminster Abbey, the Tower of London and in Chancery Lane. They were then all consolidated into one secure fireproof purpose building in Chancery Lane but this eventually became inadequate for the ever-increasing number of documents requiring storage. By 1973 work had started on the Kew riverside site which amongst other things had housed a hospital in the First World War and by 1996, all the records had been transferred from central London to their new home in the bunker style building which soon acquired the nickname 'Fort Ruskin'. The Archives store more than 11 million records including those created by central government and the courts of law, naval and military lists, census returns and tithe maps as well as national treasures such as Domesday Book and Magna Carta.

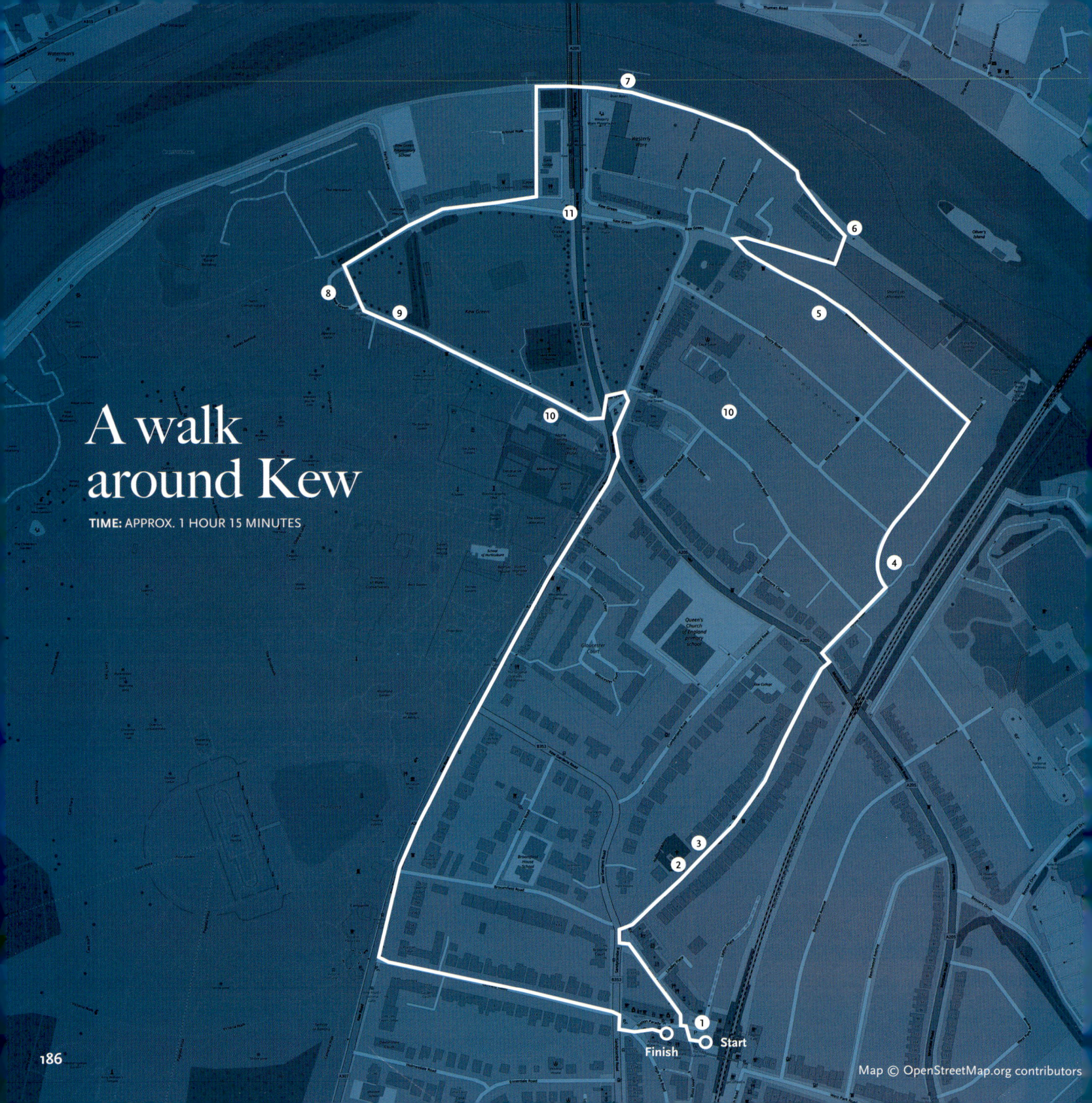

A walk
around Kew

TIME: APPROX. 1 HOUR 15 MINUTES

The walk starts outside the *Tap on the Line* pub (1) beside Kew Garden station's exit for the Royal Botanic Gardens. Walk down Station Approach past the Kew Bookshop and on reaching Sandycombe Road, glance across the road where there is a sign pointing down Atwood's Alley. This would have originally been a path running between the market gardens belonging to the Atwood family who for several generations grew fields of peas, rhubarb and celery here. Turn right into Leyborne Park. Many of the first houses in this road have elegantly tiled porches (3) and colourful glass in their front doors and were built around the turn of the twentieth century when the market garden land gave way to homes. On the left is the imposing red brick 1906 Roman Catholic church of Our Lady of Loreta and St. Winefride (2), whilst at the end of the road, Leyborne Lodge is a reminder that Frederick Atwood, a descendent of the market garden family, lived here when he was surveyor for the Leyborne Popham estate and when it was sold he would have been responsible for the layout of the new roads and also their names.

Cross the busy South Circular at the lights and take Forest Road (4) just to your right, which has some of the earliest commuter houses built in the 1880s. They have gardens but as the station was within easy walking distance, there was no need for stabling and the motor car had yet to be invented. The road has an interesting bend due to it once being part of the drive to Kew Priory. It was home to Miss Doughty, a rich and benevolent lady who owned considerable land in the area. Follow the bendy road, turn left into Bushwood Road but pause outside number 14 (5). It was once the family home of Alexander Riach who was a skilled mason working on the building of the third Kew Bridge in 1900. He was killed when a crane fell on him. Thomas Graham Menzie, an engineer, lived at number 17 and gave evidence at the subsequent inquest. The road leads to Kew Green where the now enclosed medieval fish pond remains. Once a creek linked it to the river and Henry VIII would disembark from his barge here and travel on to his palace at Richmond by horse, rather than taking the slower river route round the bend of Kew.

Do a hard right into Watcombe Cottages, a delightful terrace of artisan cottages built in 1887 on former meadow land. For years they were subject to frequent flooding. On reaching the allotments, a footpath to the left leads to the river where there is a spectacular view (6) across to Strand on the Green. Turn left and follow the tow path past the Toll House with its distinctive markings around the windows. Until 1859 London's grand City Barge Maria Wood was moored alongside here. During the 19th century the Layton family earned a living from the river carrying goods and passengers, whilst the Humphreys collected tolls and hired leisure boats. Once upon a time, the boatman's fare to take you across the water

to Brentford was one halfpenny. Lightermen with their laden barges and watermen with wherries no longer call at Kew Pier (7) but during summer months, pleasure boats with their cargo of day trippers continue to stop on their journey from Westminster to Hampton Court and back again.

When you have gone under Kew Bridge where poor Alexander Riach tragically lost his life, immediately turn left where a sign indicates the way to "Kew Gardens" and so enter the Green where cows grazed until the early 19th century. The timbered corner building is currently an Ask (11) restaurant but in 1772 it was known as the King's Arms and rebuilt in mock Tudor form, when the third bridge arrived in 1903. Capel House next door is a reminder of wealthy Lady Elizabeth Capel who was married to Samuel Molyneux, Secretary to the Prince of Wales. When he fell ill in 1728 he came under the care of Dr. Nathaniel St. André, who practiced surgery even though he had received no formal medical training and seems to have been more accomplished as a musician and dancing master. Molyneux died and his widow immediately eloped with St. André and never returned to Kew again. The Cricketers was the Rose and Crown when it opened back in 1738 and claims to be the oldest pub in Kew, although the current building only dates from the 1930s.

Imposing Georgian Hunter House forms part of the Kew Gardens Herbarium and Library and acquired the name when bought by Robert Hunter in 1800. It was subsequently known as Hanover House when home to the Duke of Cumberland, who became King of Hanover in 1837. After his death the property became part of Kew Gardens. In the Herbarium, plants are identified, named and classified. It now houses more than seven million specimens from all regions of the world, whilst the library

contains more than 750,000 volumes. The Main Gate (8) to Kew Gardens was designed by Decimus Burton in 1846 and became Elizabeth Gate to commemorate the Queen's Diamond Jubilee in 2012.

Standing on the corner of the Green is a lone green pipe. This is a Victorian sewer ventilation pipe often called a stink pipe, which allows potentially lethal gas to escape into the atmosphere. It is now Grade II listed, as is the nearby lamp stand and telephone box. The blue plaque on number 49 tells us that both Sir William Hooker (10) and his son Joseph lived here. Sir William, an eminent botanist, was appointed the first Director of Kew Gardens in 1841. Under his direction, there was expansion of the gardens and the addition of several new glass houses. This resulted in visitor numbers increasing from 9,174 in 1841 to 28,139 some four years later until 1883, when they had reached a staggering 1,244,161. When he died in 1865 he ensured that his son Joseph, also a botanist and friend of Charles Darwin, succeeded him and both father and son are buried side by side in the graveyard of nearby St. Anne's church.

Cambridge Cottage was so named when the Duke and Duchess of Cambridge lived here in 1838, preferring a home overlooking the hustle and bustle of the Green to the solitude of Richmond Park. They added the impressive stone carriage porch or porte-cochère to the front and when their son died in 1904, leaving no heirs, Edward VII gave the property to Kew Gardens to serve as a Museum of Forestry.

Royalty have been generous to the Parish Church of St. Anne ever since Queen Anne donated the land on which it is built. George III paid for the original chapel to be extended, William IV covered the costs of increasing the church's capacity by 200 seats and on the death of the Duke of Cambridge in 1851, the mausoleum with a semi-domed apse was built at the east end. In 1902 a new choir vestry was added as a memorial to Queen Victoria and in more recent times a new hall commemorates the reign of our own Queen. In the churchyard you will find the tomb of William Aiton, regarded as the first true keeper of the nearby Royal Garden; those of Hooker, father and son; and also painters Thomas Gainsborough and Johan Zoffany. Another two painters lived close by but are not buried here; Arthur Hughes was one of the Pre-Raphaelite fraternity and died at number 22 Kew Green, whilst Camille Pissarro stayed just twenty yards away on the corner of Gloucester Road and painted several local scenes, including cricket being played here on Kew Green.

Where the Green meets the busy junction of Kew and Mortlake Roads, cross carefully and go right along Kew Road, past James's Cottages, tucked down a turning on the left, and on to Gloucester Court. It is on the site of Gloucester House, once the summer residence of one of George III's brothers and part of the former estate of the Engleheart family, major landowners in this part of Kew. The charming Maids of Honour tea shop is a tempting place to stop and sample the dainty curd pastry tart of that name which has been made to a secret recipe since Henry VIII's time. The current shop opened in 1870 and was rebuilt after it was severely bombed in World War II.

Continue along Kew Road and ahead soaring above the Garden walls is the 107ft high campanile which was built in 1840 to disguise a water tower and chimney for the new Palm House to which it is connected by a tunnel. At the Victoria Gate, turn left into Lichfield Road. It is named after George Selwyn, Bishop of Lichfield – the Selwyns were also great land owners in the area. Many of these splendid Victorian villas were built soon after Kew station opened and visitors walked past them on their way to the Gardens. On number 15 is a blue plaque to Barbara Everett, an early film actress who once lived here. Straight ahead is Kew station where this walk ends.
Walk devised by Caroline MacMillan
www.westlondonwalks.co.uk

Royal Botanic Gardens, Kew

The origin of the Royal Botanic Garden can be traced back to Sir Henry Capel who created an exotic garden at his Kew Park home in the late seventeenth century. When Frederick, Prince of Wales, himself a keen gardener, leased the Park, he improved and enlarged the grounds and was planning to build a new glasshouse when he died suddenly in 1751. His widow, Augusta, continued his work with the aid of the Earl of Bute, and William Chambers was engaged to build several structures including the Chinese pagoda. William Aiton, a much-respected gardener, effected many improvements to the newly established botanical garden.

By the time William Hooker was appointed director in 1841 the gardens had suffered from some neglect but under his leadership he not only improved them but also extended their size considerably, redesigned the Orangery, created new vistas, built a new Palm House and Temperate House and the Arboretum was laid out. In addition, the Herbarium collection was founded. Under Queen Victoria's patronage the gardens flourished and with the arrival of the railway, the stream of visitors turned into a flood.

Despite two world wars, the Tea House being burned down by suffragettes in 1913 and the great storm of October 1987 when hundreds of trees were lost, the garden has continued to develop as well as taking a leading role in habitat and biodiversity conservation worldwide. In 2003 it was designated a UNESCO World Heritage Site.

Top: Sir William Hooker chose Decimus Burton to design his Palm House whilst engineer William Turner built what is Kew's most recognisable building. When it opened in 1848 it was the first large-scale structure built using wrought iron and Burton based his technology on shipbuilding, resulting in the gigantic glass house taking the shape of an upturned hull. With a rain forest climate, it houses a unique collection of palms and tropical species from around the world, some of them from the most threatened environments. They are grouped geographically though the highest palms dominate the centre of the building. It is the world's most notable Victorian glass and iron structure and despite its size, is the most gentle and graceful of buildings.

Opposite bottom left: Tucked away in the south west corner of the Gardens, the 18th century Queen's Cottage is a hidden gem and surrounded by one of London's finest bluebell woods. The cottage was a private haven for Queen Charlotte and her ladies, for resting and taking refreshments during their walks. An adjacent paddock was known as the New Menagerie and housed many exotic creatures. These included a pair of black swans, buffaloes, the now extinct quagga – similar to a zebra – and also the first kangaroos to arrive in England. On one of my many visits to Kew, I bumped into a friend, Juliette (on the left), who as well as being a member of the photographic club I run, also works at Kew and regularly dresses up in period costume, either at Kew Palace, or as pictured here at Queen Charlotte's cottage.

At the time of the restoration of Charles II, hunting was a popular sport and there were some 2,000 deer contained in the walled park. Nowadays, there are around 350 fallow and 300 red deer. During the eighteenth century, swathes of golden gorse provided thorny cover for a flock of more than 3,000 wild turkeys which were raised as game birds.

THE WAY

Believed to have been a Bronze Age burial chamber, the steep mound in Pembroke Lodge Gardens was originally known as The King's Standing and used as a vantage point for falconry and hunting. It acquired its current name due to a tale involving King Henry VIII. The story goes that he stood here on 19 May 1536, to see a rocket launched at the Tower of London to signal the execution of his wife, Anne Boleyn. However, this is unlikely as it is recorded that the king spent the evening far away in Wiltshire. The panoramic view to distant St. Paul's Cathedral has been faithfully preserved over the centuries but is now threatened by a towering block built in east London.

The Isabella Plantation

The origin of the Isabella Plantation dates back to 1831 when Lord Sidmouth fenced 42 acres of the Isabella Slade and planted them with oak, beech and sweet chestnut trees grown as a crops for timber. The transformation into today's garden of clearings, ponds and streams was the inspiration of the park superintendent George Thomson and his head gardener Wally Miller, who created it between 1951 and 1971. Work continues on a regular basis: the wild stream in the northern part has now been colonized by ferns and water plantains and the Bog Garden was reconstructed earlier this century. It is at its peak late April and early May, when the azaleas are at their flowering best.

Pembroke Lodge

When the Countess of Pembroke persuaded King George III to lease her Hill Lodge in the 1780s, it had come a long way from its humble origins as Molecatcher's Cottage. By 1847 the much-extended Pembroke Lodge was granted to the Prime Minister, Lord John Russell, and it remained in the family until 1929. It was the childhood home to philosopher Bertrand Russell and during World War II, it served as the officers' mess and billet for GHQ Liaison Regiment, known as 'Phantom'. Actor David Niven was Major of 'A' Squadron and wrote later *"These were wonderful days which I would not have missed for anything."*

Pen Ponds

Pen Ponds date back to 1746 and were formed when a trench was dug to drain a boggy area. This was later deepened by the extraction of gravel for local building. For many years the ponds were used to raise carp for food and they continue to be a haven for wildlife both in and out of the water.

227

London 10 Mile Run

As a way of attracting much needed funds for maintenance, the park closes on several days a year to hold sporting events. A new one for 2017 was the London 10 Mile Run, which attracted many thousands of runners, including my niece (top left and right inset).

There are many other running events that take place in the borough each year, one of the biggest is the Richmond RunFest, which takes place in September in Old Deer Park and uniquely, Kew Gardens. In 2016, as well as my niece Mel taking part so did my nephew Oli (left inset).

PRINTS FOR SALE

If you would like any of the pictures from this book as either a framed or unframed print or a canvas, please contact the publisher at *www.wildlondon.co.uk* where all the details can be found.

This goes for any of the books from the *Wild About* series which are shown opposite.

Other books in the Wild About series

Other books in the Wild About series by Andrew Wilson are available
to buy from all good book stores including all branches of Waterstones

Richmond Office

Second Edition – ©Unity Print and Publishing Limited 2022

History Consultant: Caroline MacMillan
www.westlondonwalks.co.uk

Designed by Kieran Metcalfe of Ascent Creative ascent-creative.co.uk

Proofreading: Amy Wilson (Pictured above with her dad, Andrew Wilson).

Printed by Matsis Global Print Solutions Istanbul
www.matsisprint.com

Colour Management by Paul Sherfield of The Missing Horse Consultancy
www. missinghorsecons.co.uk

Published by Unity Print and Publishing Limited,
18 Dungarvan Avenue,
London SW15 5QU
Tel: +44 (0)20 8487 2199
aw@unity-publishing.co.uk
www.unity-publishing.co.uk

Most of the pictures in this book were taken using a Canon 6D plus lenses with some additional shots taken using an iPhone 7.

Thank you to all the staff at Chestertons, Richmond and Kew offices, for their kind support of this book.

Richmond Office

23a Friars Stile Road, Richmond
Surrey TW10 6NH

Tel: 020 3758 3222

Kew Office

306 Sandycombe Road, Kew
Surrey TW9 3NG

Tel: 020 8104 0340

Kew Office

CHESTERTONS

www.chestertons.com

Follow Andrew on Twitter and Instagram @WildLondonPics

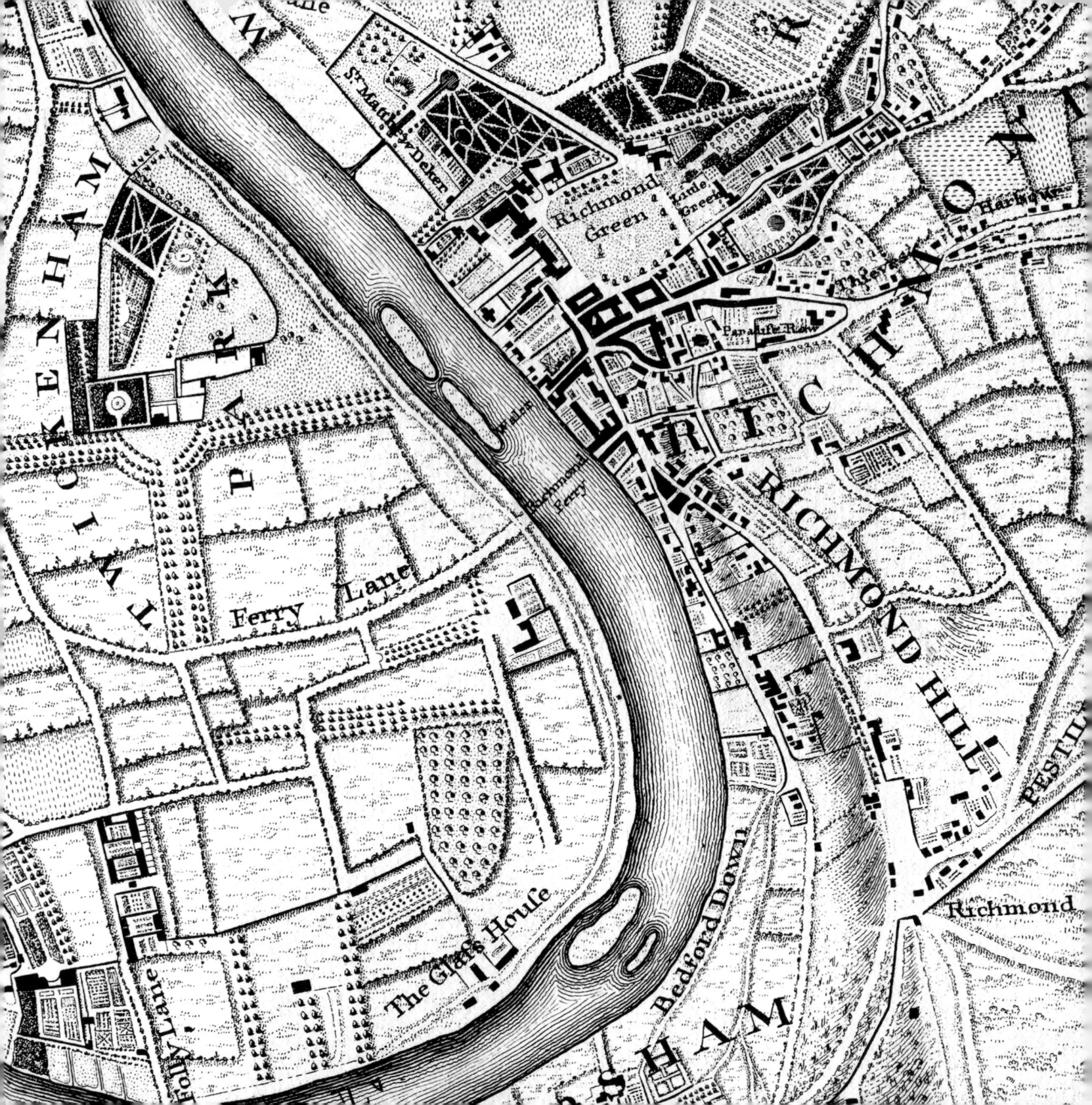